Advance F
Technology

Advance Praise from Sue Cannon:

<u>Spiritual Technology of Distance Healing</u> is a book that motivates the need within you to learn more. As you read the stories it becomes real to you. You want to put new practices to work as you feel, "I can do that too."

I feel that we all need to know about the Divine Laws of the Universe and how to be in agreement with the Laws. Alexandra has put everything in simple terms so anyone can understand and reach their highest potential.

I have practiced distance healing for many years and I know it works. Alexandra has added a few stories about my experiences that you will find in her book. I love the way she helps you understand that you can heal the ones you love even if they live hundreds of miles away, and how easy it is for anyone to apply Spiritual Technology in their everyday life.

Sue was a college recruiter and Manager of Training for Ford Motor Company; now retired.

Advance Praise from Dr. Kevin Fischer

In this book, Alexandra Alexander gifts us with a masterful tome of Distance Healing, written for both layman and experts.

Interest in the subject of spiritual healing, especially in relation to the quantum field, has exploded in recent years. Until now, what has been conspicuously absent from the literature is a practical guide on how to direct healing energy from HERE to THERE in the quantum field, whether "there" happens to be in the next city, next country, or continent.

Known for her success in healing loved ones the world over, whether those loved ones happen to belong to the plant, animal, or human kingdoms (as well as bodies of water like the Gulf of Mexico), Alexandra deconstructs the mystery of how this form of healing works and knowledgeably guides the reader step-by-step in the process of actualizing energy, concentrating energy, and directing numinous healing energy to its intended recipients, wherever they may be.

The author's fervent hope is that she can help to create a groundswell the world over, of like-minded conscientious and caring people working together for the betterment/healing of Mother Earth and all life entities contained therein.

....A thoroughly fascinating and enjoyable subject written by one of the true spiritual leaders of our time.

To: Dani & Randy
Dare to be different
Believe in the impossible.

Spiritual Technology
Of Distance Healing

Love & Light

Alexandra

Alexandra Alexander

BALBOA
PRESS

A DIVISION OF HAY HOUSE

Balboa Press books may be ordered through booksellers or by contacting:

Balboa Press
A Division of Hay House
1663 Liberty Drive
Bloomington, IN 47403
www.balboapress.com
1 (877) 407-4847

Because of the dynamic nature of the Internet, any web addresses or links contained in this book may have changed since publication and may no longer be valid. The views expressed in this work are solely those of the author and do not necessarily reflect the views of the publisher, and the publisher hereby disclaims any responsibility for them.

The author of this book does not dispense medical advice or prescribe the use of any technique as a form of treatment for physical, emotional, or medical problems without the advice of a physician, either directly or indirectly. The intent of the author is only to offer information of a general nature to help you in your quest for emotional and spiritual well-being. In the event you use any of the information in this book for yourself, which is your constitutional right, the author and the publisher assume no responsibility for your actions.

Any people depicted in stock imagery provided by Shutterstock are models, and such images are being used for illustrative purposes only. Certain stock imagery © Shutterstock.

Printed in the United States of America.

ISBN: 978-1-4525-1957-9 (sc)
ISBN: 978-1-4525-1958-6 (hc)
ISBN: 978-1-4525-1959-3 (e)

Library of Congress Control Number: 2014913882

Balboa Press rev. date: 8/22/2014

Acknowledgements

To Diana O'Hara

Thank you for being my first spiritual teacher
who opened the door to Reiki Healing.
Thank you for teaching me how to think for
myself and trust my own judgment.
Thank you for my first activation into spiritual apprenticeship.

To Sonora my mentor and friend

Thank you for assisting in removing the veil between my perceived
self and the real me; setting me free to live the life I was born to live.
Thank you for the knowledge you shared which brought
me to a comfortable place of spiritual enlightenment.
Thank you for unraveling the old dogma and reweaving
a substantial foundation of God Truths.
Thank you for believing in my abilities long
before I understood I had abilities.
Thank you for your patience as I learned to
see beyond our conscious existence.
Thank you for all your love and support.

To my family and friends

Thank you for lovingly giving your spare time to read the unfinished
version of <u>Spiritual Technology of Distance Healing</u> more than once.
Thank you for your clear suggestions and valued opinions.
Without your feedback this book would never become the
valuable asset it's to become to the Universal Light of God.

Contents

TEN MOST FREQUENTLY ASKED QUESTIONS ABOUT DISTANCE HEALING

Introduction

PLANTING THE FIRST SEEDS OF SPIRITUAL TECHNOLOGY

Off and on over the years we lived with my grandparents in Martha, Tennessee, a little town you can't find on most maps today. It's a hiccup in the road as you drive along highway 70, crossing highway 109. When I was little, Martha had a post office and not much anything else except my Uncle James' gas station where he sold bologna sandwiches and Texaco gas.

In the early fifties there wasn't as much censorship about what could be shown on TV and the little black-and-white TV in the den of my grandparents' home became my open window to the world of healing. I remember seeing a one-hour TV program presenting unusual things from all over the world. Every now and then they would show healers from other countries that within a few years would never be allowed to be shown on TV again, until the internet and YouTube came along.

As my young mind watched a healer from the Orient remove a tumor by reaching through the person's skin and pulling it out, with no incision, I was hooked. From some unknown place deep within my seven-year-old brain, I understood that I was a healer, even at such an early age. Somehow I felt as though I might be able to perform such a procedure and it didn't seem unusual as I witnessed it in black-and-white. I filed everything I saw in one of those safe places within the brain, to recall at a later time. I didn't do anything with the knowledge until I was fifty-two years old; however, I could revisit the memories stored for safekeeping. I learned about Edgar Casey, "The Sleeping Prophet" and the great pyramids of Egypt from these programs.

HOW IT ALL STARTED

In 1995 my sister Geraldine started attending meditation classes at a spirituality center called Visions of the Soul. There came such a difference in the way she reacted to life's challenges that I knew I had to investigate. It's hard for Geraldine to change, so naturally I wanted to find out what kind of miracle had taken place. I found that meditation was about getting quiet and listening to the voice within; the only trouble was staying awake while meditating in a reclined position. During those meditation classes I bumped into Reiki Healing and there was no turning back; I had found what I had been searching for over fifty years. My Soul had found its home. It was time to exhale!

After I plugged into this new enlightenment, all the glamour in the world lost its sparkle and possession of worldly things meant little. My total focus from that point forward was obligated to my Soul and anything that was Soul-related. I had no idea that Spiritual Technology was working in my life at the time. I just put one foot in front of the other, never realizing I was activating suppressed programs in the brain. Each new day became easier as I moved forward with a new understanding, diligently looking for transformational markers along the way. The first transformational marker was finding Visions of the Soul, the spirituality center in the middle of Tennessee; the second transformational marker was finding Reiki, a life-changing event; the third marker was meeting Sonora, my mentor and teacher; the fourth marker was the awakening of my spiritual gifts.

Spiritual gifts are gifts of the Spirit that some call supernatural powers. (Definition of supernatural: being above or beyond what is natural.) Having no conception of how you can "see" into the body with physical eyes or see colors swirl around people, we tend to label these abilities as something outside the natural order of life. I feel they are natural powers available to anyone who is willing to take the responsibility to activate them.

Have you ever tried to learn a foreign language? Could you talk to someone who was fluent in that language and have a good conversation after one lesson? None of us can, but that doesn't mean we can't learn to have a conversation with that person after we have mastered their language. Watching Sesame Street when my daughter was young gave me the ability to speak perfect Sesame Street Spanish. I can order a glass of agua at a restaurant, and 2113 is my la casa number and I can count from uno to diaz in Spanish. Does that make me fluent in Spanish? Do I need additional study to be proficient? Yes, I do! The same perseverance is necessary for learning a new spiritual language for the activation of your gifts. You need practice to move forward on your spiritual path.

Can you point to one gift of the Spirit within you? Did your family give you a title such as peacemaker, troublemaker, cook, artist, healer, spiritual leader, etc? I was the family artist and beautician who set the standard for spiritual behavior in our household. (Everyone got the same haircut!)

When we take on the mantle of living the spiritual life, responsibilities come with the decision. You will never find contentment in your life if you don't honor your spiritual gifts. Family members and close friends have always put me in a category of being responsible for what I wear, say and how I act towards others. I would be told in no uncertain terms when my appearance wasn't acceptable. When I let a dirty word slip from my lips, it was never met with appreciative ears. They had standards for me that they didn't follow for themselves. It felt like they knew more about me than I knew. I appreciate their loving concern for me now, but not so much when I wanted to wear a short, tight skirt. I have spent many hours pondering my role as peacekeeper, family beautician, and spiritual advisor in the family and arrived at the conclusion that it is my responsibility to be me. When we can recognize ourselves in the primordial soup of life, deciding if we are the broth that brings it all together or the peas and carrots that add to the flavor, we can better define who we are today.

We don't need a name tag saying, "I'm special;" the special part should be obvious as God flows seamlessly through our every thought, word and deed. We need to keep our deep commitment to God between us and God, and our blessings will flow through us onto others. We will be a conduit for Love.

I admit spiritual gifts come more naturally for some to activate, but I have never had a student who couldn't enhance these abilities after learning there were unrecognized gifts inside them the entire time. Once you have one gift of the Spirit open to you, many others fall from heaven as you fulfill your Sacred Contracts here on planet earth. I have been blessed by my spiritual connection to the Light and made aware of all my gifts that had lain dormant for years. The energies of high vibrational Light will assist you in becoming whoever you are meant to be. It's like winning the lottery, but first you have to buy a ticket. There has to come a time when you put forth an action to gets results. It's like the old joke about the blonde who kept praying every day, "God, why don't you let me win the lottery?" After months of hearing her pleas over and over, God finally spoke in a booming voice from heaven, "BUY A TICKET!"

We are responsible for making this simple effort in order to put things in motion. "Buying a ticket" allows dormant areas of the brain to activate programs necessary to make it happen. We must believe that we have the ability to connect to a supernatural way of living. Supernatural living is an equal opportunity state of existence that's steeped in Spiritual Technology.

One of the greatest thrills of being a teacher is assisting others in awakening to their highest potential. Seeing them grow into spiritual powerhouses, realizing I am the conductor in their lives, not the instrument or music being played, makes my heart sing. Many of my students excel past anything I am able to accomplish. Beloved Master Jesus said: "Everything I do, you can do and even greater than these." He was talking to you and me.

By 1997 my life made a ninety-degree turn. I ran away from home and left behind everything I had known for over fifty years and stepped into the unknown. I knew I had fulfilled one or two Sacred Contracts and was in the middle of a paradigm shift. (Definition of a paradigm shift: Something that does not just happen, but is driven by agents of change.) I can't say that I had a perfect plan for moving forward in this new world of healing, but I knew I had to move forward or die. It was that important to me! Surrendering was the first step; then I was carried along by an invisible force larger than myself.

I don't recommend everyone do what I did or the way I did it, but I do encourage you to follow your dreams and respond to any nudges from Spirit. Yes, I had lessons to learn along the way, especially about whom to trust. I also learned how to trust myself in making the best decisions for my future. It's great to ask others for guidance, but the ultimate decision should always be yours.

What is Spiritual Technology?

Definition of Spiritual: relating to, or affecting the human spirit or soul, as opposed to material or physical things.

Definition of Technology: the application of scientific knowledge for practical purposes.

Spiritual Technology is science and spirituality coming together in balanced harmony. It's when we can allow reasoning and believing to be compatible elements within our consciousness. We find there is no division after we remove all the cobwebs, junk and debris of dogmatic thought about spirituality and technology that has accumulated over the last ten thousand years. It's realizing there is more for us to know and understand than we have been exposed to in this lifetime. It's letting go of all ancient teachings associated with what is spiritual and gently slipping into the quantum field. You're not losing your connection to God; you're finding it! The more I understand this truth, the more I feel connected to a Divine Source of God Light.

In quantum reality you can take a leap of faith from one known point to the point of change that is already connected in your sea of quantum fields. When the wave function collapses (the state of all possibilities), a new dream becomes reality. When the particles reformulate into a wave once again, while mixing with virtual particles, a new creation is apparent; you have just activated Spiritual Technology in your world.

We all have the ability within to activate Spiritual Technology. The activation happens when we are willing to let go of what we know and embrace what feels right and natural. You can do it! Let out a rebel yell as you run through the streets of your mind and dare to be different.

> *"The heart is the means by which the soul nourishes itself." (Aristotle)*

TOROIDAL FIELD OF THE HEART

The heart's electromagnetic field—by far the most powerful rhythmic field produced by the human body—not only envelops every cell of the body but also extends out in all directions into the space around us. The cardiac field can be measured several feet away from the body by sensitive devices.

The heart has its own brain and works with the subconscious to store memories as programs until we are spiritually ready to remember. As memories surface with each program that is recognized, we have the divine opportunity to forgive and reset to a higher frequency of belief. The heart plays a larger role in our evolution than we have previously thought.

> Every thought in the human mind sends an electromagnetic wave through the heart into the electromagnetic field around us.

SPIRITUAL TECHNOLOGY HOLDS THE GPS CODE TO THE QUANTUM FIELD

When you understand the divine principles of the universe and how they work you can understand miracles. Many of the things we call miracles today are the work of Spiritual Technology. Once at zero point you are at the state of all possibilities as you are in a place that Edgar Casey called "No Time." Gregg Braden calls it the "Divine Matrix" and most scientists in the quantum field call it "Zero Point." There is no past, present or future; everything exists at the same time. Now if you can allow your mind to gently wrap around that statement you will be well on your way to miraculous Sundays, Mondays, Tuesdays, Wednesdays, Thursdays, Fridays, and Saturdays. Your good never stops once you tap into this unlimited source of potential. All it lacks is your consciousness aligning by being in agreement with whatever is showing up in your world. Our tendency is to push the river instead of going with the flow. Spiritual Technology is flowing seamlessly through whatever is appearing in your world.

PARADIGM SHIFT IN HEALING

Until we experience something, it is purely intellectual. Scientists can't explain consciousness and matter alone will not tell us what consciousness is made of. If the scientific mind can't explain consciousness, can't you see why we may have difficulty believing the unlimited possibilities available in the invisible world around us?

There has been a paradigm shift in healing over the past few years and it's on a quantum level. I don't know about you, but quantum physics was never mentioned around our dinner table. We were country folks and we talked about the weather, pan-fried potatoes, and pass-the-pickle-relish, please. We never discussed anything about a quantum particle changing because it is being observed. When I first started hearing about quantum healing there was nothing stored in my brain cells that allowed instant understanding about what was being said; there wasn't the least bit of information my mind could hold onto. I had to hear it over and over for something to take hold and make sense. That's why I understand the glassy look in people's eyes after hearing me talk about how easy it is to quantum shift into another reality; the reality they truly want in their world. They just stare at me when I try to explain that all they have to do is realize where they are and then shift into where they want to be. It seems too easy for them to understand it possibly happening.

QUANTUM LINGO

When we pin something down, when we give it a name, we freeze the particles in place and they become a projection of our imagination. We become the creator! This situation can be very beneficial if we are willing to shift our consciousness and accept a different reality or we will create another Groundhog Day experience, over and over. We get caught on the wheel and don't have the ability to find an exit. Just think of what we can do when we realize there is a construct present as we observe the wave and we have the power to collapse the construct into particles by this act of observation, which produces virtual particles in its wake. I strongly feel the virtual particles are God-particles with the ability to produce miracles. When the wave reconstructs itself you can have the same thing or you can change your thoughts and have something that you truly wish. With this virtual aspect present we have the opportunity to create beyond our wildest imagination as we apply the Divine Principles of Spiritual Technology with new creative thoughts.

4

WHY SUCH CONFUSION?

Quantum information causes a little confusion with the brain when we hear quantum terminology. The brain knows that English is being spoken, but the part of the brain that reasons can't find anything to reason with. It just causes a headache or it shuts itself down and wonders about the weather or what's for supper. So, I will keep telling you again and again until something jumps out and attaches to a brain cell getting your conscious attention. It has nothing to do with how smart we are and has everything to do with the information we have been exposed to until now. Don't take it personally or turn away from information that can be life-changing, if the first time we hear it all we want to do was say, "poppycock" and take a nap.

ORDINARY CIRCUMSTANCES EVOLVE INTO EXTRAORDINARY EVENTS

I had never heard of Wesak in 1996, and had no idea what it was and no Internet at the time to Google the event. However, Diana, my spiritual teacher, had scheduled a speaker to bring the energies and information of Wesak to Visions of the Soul, our spirituality center in middle Tennessee. Sonora, the speaker, arrived hours before the event and since I had volunteered to assist with the details of pulling everything together, I got to spend extra time with her. She was a small package of a woman who had the ability to project a large energy; the largest energy I had ever felt from anyone. You could feel her presence as she entered the room and the first time we met I was a little unnerved by the all-consuming way she took ownership of my space. It wasn't that she was trying to be invasive; the pure force of her light overshadowed everything and everyone around her.

I had just started cutting my teeth on the spiritual movement and was hungry to be a part of anything akin to the supernatural aspect of living. I knew Sonora was different in a good way the first time we met. You could sense something about her that was beyond the obvious; her perfect hair and clothes made you think she held an executive position of some kind, but I could tell there was more going on in her world. Sonora offered spiritual consultation sessions while she was at the center and in one hour I received guidance and answers to questions that until then had remained unanswered. Thank God, I had finally found my mentor and teacher!

PLUGGING INTO THE INNER PLANES

Distance healing is a division of inner planes work. When you open an etheric tube of Light you are using Spiritual Technology in the inner planes at zero-point level. This spiritual technique comes in handy when you wish to look at some area of your life that doesn't necessarily have anything to do with distance healing. I learned to look in and ask to see whatever was amiss in my world to get answers to bothersome questions. I also learned that I could look into the past as easily as into what was happening in the present and make corrections by forgiving myself and others. When we forgive the past we reset the frequency that held the memory in place and the vibrational shift is felt in real time. The act of forgiving allows the new pattern code to vibrate through the family line. You may not think this is a big deal, but it has larger ramifications than you can imagine. I have seen this remove harmful vibrational imprints from family lines that have happened over and over again for hundreds of years. We can be the catalyst for change benefiting the whole family. Think about it: you can change the frequency of abuse running through the family line so your children won't experience what you experienced. Any kind of crazy that runs deep through the family line can be changed.

HERE'S HOW I DID IT

Sonora introduced me to the inner planes and helped me hone the skill of looking in to see things on other levels of existence. During conversations with Sonora I would discuss what was going on in my life, sometimes seeking advice. If I had a question, she would ask me to look in and tell her what I could see. The first time I didn't see anything. I just sat there and thought, "I don't see jack!" She would keep saying, "Look again and tell me what you see," speaking in an even tone of voice. Not knowing exactly what I was supposed to see, I had no results. Then with a more authoritative tone she would say, "TELL ME WHAT YOU SEE!" It shocked me so badly that it took me out of my conscious state to someplace new and different; immediately I could see the image necessary to answer my question. That first experience planted a seed in my subconscious that allowed new neural pathways to form in my brain center, causing an advanced program code to be activated. I was well on my way to understanding Spiritual Technology.

PERSEVERANCE PAYS OFF

We create neural pathways through our experiences as we download them into the brain center. The first time creates a path to the neural networkings of the brain, and after a few of the same experiences a new stable path is created giving us access over and over again. The same as when we learned to tie our shoes. Were you proficient when you first looped the rabbit ears of your laces? More than likely you were just like the rest of us and had to do it over and over before you had a solid pathway in your neural network to open the program to tie your shoes. Once the program is solidly in place you don't even have to think; it opens the second you touch a shoestring. The same goes for not falling out of bed, walking across the floor or riding your bike without the training wheels. They are all programs you installed with the help of others as you learned to accomplish each task. Just like learning these simple tasks, you have the ability to give those dormant brain cells something to do as each experience imprints itself into new pathways in the brain center, awakening the sleeping potential within.

APPLIED SPIRITUAL TECHNOLOGY

Do you know how some injured ball players or golfers become more proficient in their game while injured and unable to play? They have learned that programming the subconscious with their conscious mind is just as powerful as the physical act. The subconscious will believe a lie just as quickly as the truth and that's how wishes become real. If they have trouble with a skill all they do is imagine it the way they want it to happen over and over in their mind; when they are healed and ready to apply the physical action into the game, they are better than before. I read that Tiger Woods "sees" the golf ball go into the hole before he ever swings his club. You can use this process with anything in your life. I found that I could do this in my artwork. When I needed to draw an object I would sit and concentrate until I could see it in my mind's eye clearly. When I drew the object as a physical action it came out perfectly. All the above results are a part of Spiritual Technology. It becomes part of our everyday life as we tap into that unknown part of ourselves and utilize zero-point energy.

In my catering days I started decorating wedding cakes and found that I had a problem with the reverse shell border that goes around the edge of the cake. It made a beautiful design on the cake, but the harder I tried the bigger mess I made. It was like rubbing your tummy and patting your head at the same time. You had to move the pastry bag to the right and then switch to the left. I am not sure why this was such a challenge, but it was my nemesis for about a month. I put it aside and from time to time I would think about that shell border and how the pastry bag in my hands would swing back and forth and a beautiful shell design would emerge and caress the edge of the cake. One day, I picked up the pastry bag and almost like magic, the reverse shell appeared from the tip of that pastry bag as I gracefully laced the reverse trim around the cake. It was the most beautiful thing I had ever seen. I was amazed in one respect and then totally aware of my thinking about doing it before I actually made it. I knew I had created that automatic action by thinking about it over and over. I combined science and technology by believing in myself and achieved favorable results.

> Mary Kay Ash, founder of Mary Kay Cosmetics always said, "If you can believe it, you can achieve it!" I believe she was right.

IS DAVID COPPERFIELD BEHIND THE DOOR?

If we trust ourselves and believe in our abilities we can create the world around us that we desire. First we need a plan and then we need to stir in some belief. It's that simple! When we know what it is and put our trust into the plan, poof! It happens, just like magic; but it isn't magic, its science. It's the creative process of the Universe that we have tapped into using Spiritual Technology. We will feel as though every hat we see contains a rabbit, waiting for us to pull it out and amaze the crowd. It's just science waiting for us, the scientist, to open the secrets of the universe.

Scientists say that genius may be our better ability to access the Field. Einstein would take a nap to access the Field and solve a problem. Edgar Casey would go into a trance to access the Field. Nicola Tesla meditated to access the knowledge in the Field.

I tell my students that all we need is the architect's drawing, not the completed house when manifesting a dream. Getting out of the way of the energies of God that are present in our life allows a divine creation to take place. Allowing the Light of God to fill in all the blank places to bring joy and satisfaction into our world creates our bliss. There is always an intelligent presence available to take care of the nuts and bolts of life; when we allow God to fill in the blanks, Spiritual Technology is being used.

PUTTING THE DIVINE PRINCIPLES OF THE UNIVERSE TO WORK

There are three requirements that must be acknowledged:

1. There are certain rules that must be obeyed.
2. There is a Divine Directive in place at all times.
3. There is an Intelligence that must always be recognized

If we follow the Universal template and obey the basic rules, we will exhibit what some would call magical powers. I call them Supernatural Powers and we all have the ability to access these Powers. Only a few know how to activate the code of Universal Intelligence that gives us access to the Divine Principles of the Universe, creating our heaven on earth. My desire is for all to know that we have within us everything it takes to live a full Supernatural Lifestyle.

The Intelligence present in the Divine Intelligence of the Universe is the presence of God. When we align with the Intelligence, being in agreement we form a symbiotic relationship. There is no way to separate ourselves from God. Once we are in agreement we establish a code of Oneness that not only benefits us, but everyone who is seeking Oneness. If we can exhibit the ability to achieve Oneness, others will understand the possibilities of living a full God-connected Divine existence.

We must realize the presence of God in any action taking place around us at all times. No matter what is showing up, God is present!

We may ask, "What's up with that, God?" while we are picking up the broken glass. God is present! God is always present! Believe that the Light of God will always give us an answer to whatever form of crazy is showing up in our world, if we are sincere about the question.

The secret code that gives us access into the Divine Universal Light is our frequency of belief. The Light will clarify our frequency and plug us into the God-code necessary for whatever is needed at any given time. We have to step outside of everything we know about prayers and miracles as we merge into the intelligent stream of Divine Universal Principles flowing through the quantum Field. We are not "The Power"; we have become a *part* of the "Power." Once the intimacy of our union is understood we can reach our highest state of enlightenment.

The rules are not hard to follow; however, we are not allowed to deviate from the original system that is in place. There is a consequence if we use this information selfishly; it must always be for the good of the whole. The power we access must never be used as power over others. We are responsible for our connection to the Light; no one else can access the space for us. We are obligated to take responsibility for every creation that shows up in our world whether good or bad. Our success rate for working in the Universal Light diminishes if we deny what is showing up around us, as our stuff. Belief is the most important element necessary for success in the field. If we can't believe we have the ability to change weather, we never will. If we can't believe that healing cancer is possible we will never receive a healing. If we can't believe that we have within us the code to connect to the Universal Light, we will never access the dimensional systems, necessary for Supernatural activity. To be effective in the Light we must believe we are capable before we experience validation. We then move out of our conscious mind into the Mind of God. Then and only then is when we recognize we are in that space-time continuum where everything exists at once and miracles are an everyday occurrence of daily life.

EXAMPLE OF PUTTING THE DIVINE
PRINCIPLES OF THE UNIVERSE TO WORK

A few years ago a good friend of mine attended her thirtieth high school reunion where she reunited with an old friend, which eventually led to making wedding plans. Because I had twenty years of catering experience creating beautiful receptions for hundreds of weddings, I offered to help. It was to be an outdoor event at a private residence in Georgia. This meant the cake and the crowd would be exposed to the elements.

When I first saw the house and grounds I held my breath, it was so breathtakingly beautiful. I couldn't believe the hostess cared for the grounds by herself without any help. (However, she did have a great tan!) There was a stunning in-ground swimming pool behind the house, and down a sloping ridge in the manicured lawn was a manmade lake that hugged the back of the property. As I walked down terraced steps of slate I got the full view of the lake, with fountains spaced across the surface. The azaleas that bordered the back yard were close to seven feet tall.

To the left of the property was an area with trees that had been cleared of underbrush. The hostess had made little trails that led to meditation spots, with each little hideaway containing a wrought-iron bench or chairs. She had placed hanging baskets of bougainvillea that cascaded to the ground, adding a burst of color to the area. There were a few multicolored blankets of impatiens that benefited from the spackled light coming through the trees that were a delight to see. The whole area had a strong pull, urging me to walk one of the trails and sit awhile to commune with nature.

The wedding day arrived and so did the rain clouds. The bride's daughters and brother came to her with concern about the weather. They were all worried about the forecast for heavy rains that could ruin everything. They tried to talk her into cancelling the outdoor ceremony and move to a local church. After they went back to the house the bride and I surveyed the setting. A beautiful wedding arch covered with flowers faced the lake along with 100 gleaming white chairs spaced in neat rows waiting for the guests to arrive.

We could feel a mist of rain starting to fall. The bride and I decided not to panic and said prayers for a beautiful outcome. We gratefully thanked God for any and all assistance we could receive to make an outdoor wedding possible. We thanked the clouds for retaining their water and explained how important the day was to the bride. We honored all energies present and gave thanks for being a part of the prayer. We honored the elements and the elemental energies that cared for the property.

After the prayer the bride got dressed in her beautiful lace gown and walked down the grass covered aisle toward the lake. It was simply beautiful. We didn't know until after the ceremony that there was a deluge all around the subdivision. The skies had opened and cried all over that part of Georgia. The guests were amazed that it wasn't raining on the wedding ceremony. The bride and I were grateful for the outcome, because nothing tastes worse than a watered-down wedding cake!

The thing to remember here is we were in agreement and grateful before we knew the outcome. We followed the rules by recognizing the Divine Presence of God, acknowledging the Divine Directive that was in place and giving recognition to any intelligence that was present. In a picture someone had taken of the bride and I a visible light attached us to some unknown space in the heavens. The bride and I gave thanks for the validation of the Divine presence of the Universal Light of God on her very special day.

I don't relate this story to make me seem like I am more special than you. I relate this story to let you know you are just as capable as I. I never, under any circumstance, use the Light of God as my soapbox to sell you on my abilities.

> We all have the ability to create happiness;
> It's an equal opportunity state of mind.

A Note: You will find some of the information being repeated over and over through the book. This is on purpose! Some of the wording about Spiritual Technology is incomprehensible to many when they hear it the first time. You may need to hear it again and again like I did. I felt like a first-grader at times when I read about quantum physics. Keep reading and soon the gobbledygook of the message will become clear.

Ten Most Frequently Asked Questions about Distance Healing

1

What Is Distance Healing?

HOW I EXPLAIN THE QUANTUM FIELD OF LIFE-FORCE

Distance healing is sending Light over any distance from one source to another through the Ethers/Quantum Field/Zero-Point Energy. The integrity of our intention is held in place as it travels to its intended destination to connect with another person receiving the Light. Everyone has a Light signature that can be initiated by saying his or her name. The connection is made through the Quantum Field by initiating the coded Light of the individual seeking healing. It's pretty simple to understand how this works once we embrace the quantum aspect of being connected to everything and everyone by an invisible force of light called Life-Force, no matter where we may be.

First we have to understand that we are working in the Quantum Field while doing distance healing. Wrapping our mind around the quantum experience necessitates accepting new thought patterns that have never existed in our consciousness. Even Einstein had issues with quantum entanglement and called it spooky action at a distance. Knowing that he was pretty smart and open-minded about a lot of things you can understand why our brains want to shut down when we hear we can send healing to anyone over great distances, and it works without our even touching them. We're in good company not knowing how things work! We need always to trust our inner feelings (gut feelings, as my granny called them) while maintaining the belief that it's real and that we need to pay attention.

Working in the Quantum Field is like moving through a pool of water. As we enter the pool we move through the water and it totally surrounds us, slouching and bending as we swim through it. We have the freedom to move in the matrix of the pool, staying connected to everyone without interfering with their connections to the pool. Life-Force is like the pool of water; it stays contained in the Universe and we move through it. There is buoyancy in the Universe just like in the pool, when you "swim" in the "sea" of Quantum Fields. Looking around the pool, we can see that everyone is connected by the same substance, freely playing or floating. The water is the medium that allows us and everyone else in the pool to stay connected as we swim from end to end. Life-Force is the same and is the medium that connects everyone at all times in the quantum pool. It doesn't matter where we are in the pool of Life-Force; we are connected by an invisible net of light.

SOME CALL IT A MATRIX

I see Life-Force as a very thick substance with a spider web appearance to its structure. Our light is connected to the Life-Force around us as we move through the structure of this Field/Matrix. We connect our light to the existing light that is present in the Field/Matrix, allowing us to send our energetic thought anywhere we can imagine. Every thought we have finds its intended contact with the energy frequency that was initiated with our thought. For instance, if we are thinking loving thoughts about someone, 90% of the time we will get a call from that person wanting to know how we are doing. I have seen this happen again and again. When someone comes for a session wanting to correct some discord with family members, we remove the embedded beliefs and do a little forgiving; by the time the session is over, the family member will be calling to check up on them. They felt the release of all the negative energy between them on a higher level and wanted to know what was going on. Making corrections within ourselves frees the other person to self-correct and forgive; we are releasing the strands of light energy that held the negative energy in place. They felt the release even though they were not present.

I use the analogy of the tug-of-war, when you are pulling one end of a rope and someone else is pulling the opposite end. The struggle is over when you drop your end of the rope. It's not any fun to stand and hold a rope. The same thing happens in life when we forgive and let go of the strings and strands that held the angers in place.

Doesn't this assist in anchoring an understanding that close proximity is not a big concern in distance healing? It's because of our quantum connection in the Field, not by how close we are standing to an individual. Literally, no matter where we are, we are connected to those we know and we can connect to those we don't know by speaking the code necessary for the connection.

MORE SIGHT ON THE INNER PLANES

In 1996, seeing on the inner planes was new territory for me and I had no idea initially what Sonora was asking me to do. I know she wanted to shake me a couple of times to get my attention, but she kept her cool and I finally started to comprehend what she was asking me to do. We have to go somewhere else in our mind to do inner planes work. Our conscious everyday minds won't get us there. We must be exposed to the idea for a program to be written within the mind centers of the brain. New neural pathways will be established for us to use again and again when we practice distance healing; but until the pathways are put in place, our conceptual view will be distorted by doubt and lack of knowledgeable experiences. The more I listened to Sonora as she patiently worked with me, the more I comprehended what she was trying to convey. I had to hear it over and over for it to make some kind of contact with that part of the brain that reasons. Don't give up when you try to look in the first time or second time or even the fiftieth time. One day it will be there for you to understand what you are seeking. Be patient and find your own Sonora to assist you along the way.

There has to come a time when we allow ourselves to go beyond the known facts and embrace a new thought without knowing everything. We have to develop a sense of discovery, a Christopher Columbus type of philosophy, not knowing everything, but being sure it will make itself available if we persevere. It's about trusting that we have what it takes to get the job done by following a good set of directions. I was astonished the first time I saw something that I had requested to see. Sonora had told me to look at a particular energy situation and sure enough, it appeared in front of me in my mind's eye. After that first experience it kept getting easier and easier each time I looked in to see what was going on in my world or the world of another.

Learning to see on the inner planes is simple to do and I know you can do it with a little practice. On your first try, find a place that is quiet; distractions will impede your ability to see. The conscious mind is curious; it wants to explore every sound and interpret every motion being made. I don't even have music playing because my conscious mind will go to the music and it keeps me from hearing effectively. I have found it's easier to practice when others are not in the house. It helps to start with a simple question that revolves around your spiritual growth. Don't ask questions like, "Is my boyfriend/girlfriend unfaithful to me?" You will have too much of your ego invested in those kinds of questions. My first questions were about the direction my life was taking and whom to trust when asking for advice. The first time Sonora asked me to look in and see something, it concerned an uneasy feeling I was having in my life, something that I was not able to look at with my conscious vision. She assisted me in seeing the answer and immediately I had peace with the situation.

There is not a lot more instruction I can give you other than you have to start somewhere to get something accomplished. The more you tied your shoes the easier it got as you made a solid program in your brain center. The more you look into the inner planes seeking answers, the more your frequencies will connect to the appropriate plug-in within your neural network. Everything is already in place waiting for you to make a solid connection by practicing with the frequency of your mind. Give your brain permission to assist you without fully understanding how or what the brain is doing. You may surprise yourself with what you are capable of doing with just a little faith in your abilities.

BEYOND OUR KNOWING

There is so much out there that is beyond our knowing. After I started seeing angels I thought I had arrived and there wouldn't be much left to impress me; this belief lasted for quite a few years. I had seriously backed into some pretty concrete beliefs about the Universe. I should have known better! Just when you think you have it all figured out is when you have to get the pencil and paper ready for new dictation from God. I know God loves me and God is unoffendable; if not I would be crispy-fried by now. Let me share with you what I learned about the Light and how the knowledge helped me to understand how distance healing works.

LIGHT EXPERIENCE AFTER MY TRIP TO PAKISTAN, APRIL 2008

We have family in Pakistan and try to go over every few years to visit. Coming home after our last visit we had a five-hour layover in New York. When I finally arrived home, I was tired beyond description. I sat in my living room exhausted and unable to go to sleep. At the time I didn't realize I was in an altered state of consciousness. Being born under the sign of Virgo, I have a very active mind that never shuts down. It took this kind of exhaustion to get my ego/conscious mind to shut down and allow my unconscious mind to take me to a place that I had never visited in this lifetime.

Being so tired I couldn't even think after our long journey, I just sat in my pink wingback chair in the living room, trying to muster the energy to get up and go to bed. In my slightly unconscious state, from the deep fatigue I was experiencing I began to notice my hands and how alive with energy they were. Not only did energy project ten or more inches from the tips of each finger, I could see light shinning from my palms and the top of my hands and around my body. I then noticed the Light that connected my Light to everything in the room. In my altered state I thought, "Wow, this is what Life Force looks like." There was a web of Light everywhere, not just around me, but connected to the chair, lamps, rug, everything. As I moved my hand around my body I could see the Light allowing me to move through without disturbing the web of Light. The web didn't seem to move, but allowed my movements to slip through the design in the Light. The web of Light did seem to have what appeared to be a breathing movement that enhanced the feeling of an Intelligent Force surrounding me.

I could see the building of a thought form directly in front of me that looked like thick white smoke. As I placed my fingers of Light into the thought form it disturbed the placement of the smoke, but it moved back into place when I removed my fingers. I repeated this a few times to see what would happen. It was the image of our outside dogs that had greeted me so robustly when I returned home. They were just sitting at my feet. I remembered thinking how glad I was to see them. I didn't know I could carry a common everyday experience like that in my energy field until that evening. I sat there reasoning that this is how a thought form attaches to our field of Light. I found that very interesting as I continued to play with the Light.

Wherever I moved my hands, they connected to the Light. I looked down at the Oriental rug and watched in amazement as the molecular structure of the rug came alive. I could see the building blocks of everything at a molecular level and was entertained quite awhile as I looked through the layers interacting with the substance in the Light. The Life-Force Energy around me looked like a thick blanket that clung to my hands and changed the clothes I was wearing. It was interesting to see the fabric of my black slacks change into little patterns of Light that would interact with the Light from my hands. Everything in the room was connected and woven together in such a fashion that is hard to describe. The thickness of it all was the most astounding thing to see. There was no space between anything. Everything was attached to or enmeshed to everything else around me. Trillions of little geometric shapes held everything together with a spider web appearance.

Why can't we see this fabric of Light that seems thick enough to cut with a knife, all the time? I don't know! I do know that it exists and is in place every moment in time. It all seemed so surreal and playing with the Light was the thing to do at that moment. I am so thankful for having this enlightening experience that helped me understand how easy it is for Light to travel from one place to another. When you witness how well-formed the web of Life-Force is around us, you stop questioning how it works and start putting it to work. Seeing it up close and personal, you understand that you are never disconnected from the Light and that it supports you in all you choose to project into the Field.

I have been a healer/teacher for many years and have seen unusual things quite often. I saw my first Indian Guide in the summer of 1996 and my first Angel Guide not long after. I see Light around people and hear voices from the other side. Unusual Light is what I am accustomed to working with in my healing practice. What I experienced on that April evening was seeing all Light working together in a cohesive manner. There is established Light, "Life-Force Energy," that connects everything and directed Light that moves within this Life-Force Energy. (The Life-Force Energy didn't seem to move.) Seeing the presence of Life-Force Energy around me made me aware of how it all works. I received an understanding of how we are connected and how the energetic streams of information connect to all Universal Light.

DO YOU WANT THE GOOD NEWS OR BAD NEWS?

Here's the bad news; whatever you think finds its destination. Your thoughts are like a heat-seeking missile and will find their target. Watch what you are thinking! Now for the good news: whatever you think will find its destination. It's good or bad according to what we are projecting with our consciousness. Working creatively in the Light means being in agreement with the Light around you and the Light you are projecting into the Field. The field mirrors to us whatever we are projecting. Stay very clear on what you want in life, unplugging from as much doubt as possible. Always recognize that you are interacting with an intelligence that is around you at all times. Acknowledging the intelligence is being in agreement with the intelligence.

I AM RESPONSIBLE FOR LETTING YOU KNOW

There comes an obligation with Spiritual knowledge that can't be ignored if you ever want to find peace. If I had gone to sleep and never had this experience I wouldn't have the responsibility of sharing this knowledge with everyone. I have entered the sanctuary of the soul by accepting the knowledge as fact; now my truth belongs to the world.

DISTANCE HEALING EXPERIENCES (INCLUDING DISTANCE IN MILES)

I have included the distance between the healer and the one receiving the distance healing to help you understand that distance doesn't matter when you are working in God's country.

COLLAPSING LEG

Distance Healing 120 miles away. In 1998 when I was still learning how distance healing worked, I started sending healing to a friend who had trouble with a leg collapsing when he tried to stand. He was on disability and had given up riding his motorcycle a few years before because he never knew when his leg would give way. I started distance healing on his leg and after about a month he was riding his motorcycle again. One of the things I had done was put his name on a piece of paper along with Reiki Symbols for distance healing and placed it in my shoe to send healing energy when I walked. I also sent energy through the absent healing symbol as I meditated on his healing. Whatever I did had an effect that was positive. At that time I was nowhere close to being an expert; I was still in the process of learning about what I was doing when sending him energy and I did what I thought would help. It doesn't take a seasoned healer to officiate a healing, it takes a willing heart. My friend received a favorable outcome from a novice.

CLEARING FAMILY FREQUENCIES

Distance Healing, 112 miles away; by my friend Brandy. Six years ago, my daughter was about to run off with a boyfriend like some teenagers will do. I was receiving instruction from friends and family that seemed to make things escalate toward the atomic bomb stage. I called Alexandra and through her guidance I was able to release the fear around what was going on. I could feel an immediate shift during our session and in one hour my whole world changed for the better. In no time that guy was out of our lives and my daughter was back in school. If I had continued to fight the energy that was present I am positive we would not have had such a perfect outcome.

When I talk to Alexandra or just think about her I can feel a pulse start in my hands and feet. During phone consultations discussing my life I can feel it affect my whole body. I know there are changes happening in my world because I can feel them as we speak. I know Reiki Healing works as I plug back into my Light, making it easier to deal with all that is happening around me. When the family knows I am about to call Alexandra, they all ask, "Are you going to talk about me today?" They always get excited and know something positive will change in their world.

My husband worked as Special Ops in the Army for over twenty years and we have had many sessions clearing him of the things he has experienced in combat. Being Special Ops means he does the things we Americans don't want to hear about; things most people never hear about. With each session we cleared him of the things he has dealt with over the years keeping him plugged into his power source of truth. I never tell him beforehand when I plan on talking to Alexandra. I wait to see if he can feel the shift in his world. He would be sleeping on the other side of the world when I am talking to her and he knew the next morning that something had changed and asks if I talked to her. He is absolutely better after each session! I find it amazing that he can clear what is out of sync by my talking with Alexandra in the USA. He values her work but wants me to talk to her.

Most of my husband's army friends have emotional problems and drink way too much. They have trouble dealing with civilian life and life in general. My husband should have PTSD; however, he is happy and healthy and I give a lot of credit to the unbelievable work with Alexandra as she assists me in plugging my Light back into my power source of God. I am amazed that my family changes through my conversations with Alexandra. She will not be speaking to them, but goes through me to them. What a gift to receive.

<hr />

Distance healing story from my friend Sue: Sue and I are good friends and have experienced extraordinary events together. I first met Sue when she came to our healing class in 1998 with a broken ankle. Classes were every Monday night and she somehow found us way out in the sticks of Mt. Juliet, Tennessee. Her ankle was swollen and trying to push its way out of the cast. We did a healing on her and all the swelling and discomfort left her ankle within fifteen minutes. I thought it was pretty cool to watch. It was like watching a deflating balloon. We have been close friends ever since.

HEALING SUE'S BROTHER

Distance healing, 1,496 miles away. Sue's brother told her he was having lots of pain in his right knee and had difficulty walking. The surgeon's diagnosis after the examination left no doubt that surgery was necessary, and it was scheduled for the next week to repair damage to the ligaments and tendons. Sue started sending distance healing a week before his surgery, not mentioning it to her brother. He called Sue three days after the surgery to tell her good news: the surgeon said the damage wasn't nearly as bad as he thought it would be. Sue gives a lot of credit to a great outcome to the distance healing. She continued to send distance healing to her brother after the surgery. Her brother hasn't had trouble with his knee since.

———•———•——

THE WORLD'S MOST UNUSUAL THERAPIST

This is an almost unbelievable story of the distance healing of criminally insane inmates in a Hawaii state hospital by Dr. Hew Len. Joe Vitale relates how he had heard about Dr. Hew Len and thought his story was an urban legend. When he finally met Dr. Hew Len the doctor told him how he Len never saw a single inmate the four years he was employed at the hospital, but only looked at the patients' files in his office. Len said he would heal himself as he looked at the patient's files while sending energy to the inmates. After a while the inmates that had been shackled were walking around freely and those that had been heavily medicated were no longer taking medications. The nurses stopped calling in sick and patients who were never to be released started going home. It was so successful that after four years the ward was closed for lack of inmates.

Len said that all he was doing to heal himself as he looked at patients' files was to keep repeating, "I'm sorry" and "I love you" over and over again.

It turns out that loving yourself is the greatest way to improve yourself, and as you improve yourself, you improve your world.

(Learn more about the Ho'oponopono prayer in Zero Limits by Joe Vitale and Hew Len.)

SENDING LIGHT TO FIDO AND KITTY KAT

Below is an email to a student utilizing her training in distance healing using the *Hon Sha Ze Sho Nen* on animals. I am very proud of her stepping out of her comfort zone and trying something different. She wanted to use Skype to send healing energies to her friend's dog that was sick and needing attention, some 60 miles away.

Email to Jen: Animals are easier to work with than humans, because you don't have to wade through their story. Animals don't have judgments like humans and they haven't made all the programs of belief that need clearing for a healing to take place. You just connect to their Light and go to work. You are working in a field of Light and can blend your Light with their Light very easily by thinking the connection has been made. You can connect to the Light of the animal by saying the name of the animal and make a connection even stronger by using the vibration of the owner. The person calling about the animal needing assistance helps in connecting to the animal, because their Light knows the Light signature of their pet. This is easy to do. Your job is to hold the Light and the image of pure health as the facilitator and be in deep gratitude for the honor of serving the Light. Remembering it's just a Divine principle you have activated, not a miracle, even though it seems like one. You are not there to heal; you are there for the healing to take place. Don't forget to smile. If on Skype just tune into the animal visually as well as their Light.

Jen had a very successful outcome using Skype to send healing energy to her friend's pet.

HOW TO INITIATE A DISTANCE HEALING FOR ANIMALS

It is so much easier to correct the frequency of distorted Light in animals than in humans. Animals don't have a belief system and they tend to work more consciously with their ultra senses. They already have better hearing and can smell anything half a mile away before we get a whiff. The most important thing is no belief system, which allows them to be in a quantum field and ready to shift instantly.

Dogs have a sense of who to trust. I rented an apartment once and didn't need to give any references because the family dog gave me a big welcome lick or two when I got out of the car to meet the landlord. After I found out about the personality of Anne the family dog I understood why. She was more scary than friendly to everyone that come on the property.

STORIES OF HEALINGS ON ANIMALS; NEAR AND FAR

Distance healing 1400 miles away: Sue's daughter called when Otto, their Great Pyrenees dog, was having trouble walking. His hip was sore and prevented him from putting weight on his hind leg. Sue told her daughter she would start that evening sending distance healing to Otto and did so twice a day. Her daughter called after ten days and told Sue that Otto could walk again and could put weight on his leg. She said, "Thank you, Mom; I believe the distance healing contributed to his healing.

———•———•——

Mother, a huge German shepherd, was my first experience of seeing the Light of an animal mix with my Light. Mother sat on the floor close to my feet as I worked on a wound she had received. As I connected to her, a shimmery purple and blue Light attached my hands to her body. I was amazed at how easy it was to see the Light travel from my hands to Mother. She healed rapidly, but it didn't improve her disposition. Mother had the tendency to make you want to climb a tree when she was around. We became fast friends after the healing and she never growled at me again. Mother is the perfect example of why it's a good thing to learn distance healing. It may also apply when thinking about your mother-in-law.

———•———•——

I was visiting a friend in Georgia a few years ago and we went to her daughter's house for a swim. After swimming for a while we dried off and went inside for soda and conversation. The daughter had two little white fluffy dogs inside and the older of the little dogs found a spot beside me and wouldn't move the whole time I was there. I knew by his seeking me out that he needed healing so I sent him Light as I gently stroked his back. After forty minutes or so we left and I said goodbye to my new furry friends. Later I heard from my friend's daughter that my little companion, who until then was having trouble jumping up on the bed, no longer had any problems and seemed like a young pup again. Dogs heal so easily and I have found that they know who is a healer and will gravitate to them if a healing is needed.

———•———•——

My brother and sister-in-law were visiting and brought their little poodle Daisy with them. Daisy's old joints needed some healing love. I worked on Daisy across the living room during the four days they were here, placing Daisy in the tube of Light; Hon Sha Ze Sho Nen. After the second day I noticed that Daisy didn't need any assistance jumping up on the sofa anymore and she seemed to sleep less. I very seldom touched her; all I did was put her in Light wherever she was in the room. Distance healing also works up close, which is good because some animals just don't like to be touched. However, they can feel what you are doing and will turn their heads and look at you in acknowledgement. Daisy did start to jump onto my lap to give me a quick "Hi" after the third day.

DISTANCE HEALING ON WILD BIRDS

When I lived on the lake there were lots of trees and water and lots of birds. Quite often birds would fly into the glassed-in porch on the second level of the house. Hearing the thud of contact brought my attention to a starling lying unconscious on the ground with its head and neck lying in an awkward position. I couldn't tell if it was alive or not, but thought it best to send Light. After a few minutes it turned its head and looked my way before flying off. I was totally amazed by the experience of interacting with this species, knowing that the bird knew I had been of assistance. Cool, huh? This became a common occurrence over the five years I lived there, so I got to experience it quite often.

Distance healing works well on all wild animals and is much safer than picking up a baby skunk or squirrel, no matter how cute they may appear.

MORE ON CATS

I can tell if the cats are healthy when I enter a home by their interaction with me. If they need healing they are on me like white on rice. Even if they don't need healing they will come and say hi as they tango around my feet. I appreciate the validation and always smile and give them a friendly rub.

Cats can smell a healer from a block away and don't have a problem letting you know what they need. When I am around a kitty needing healing energy, it will either wrap around my shoulders like a fur collar or tie my feet in a knot. Cats are funny creatures; you don't have to worry about cats being subtle. Once a cat gets all the energy it needs from you, it will leave you alone and go back to being the mysterious loner.

The size of an animal doesn't matter. I have friends who work with horses all the time and they remark on how easy the horses respond to high vibrational energy. It's a love thing and the larger they are the more you get to love. It's that simple.

Let go of any fear you may have about your abilities to sending healing Light to someone. You can't fail! Whenever you send the Light of God to anyone it has a positive effect and they will benefit from your love. The more you allow the Light to work in their Light without worry or fear, the quicker they will understand it's safe to let go of whatever their Light may be plugged into. We can change the world by our ability to Love. I am talking about sending Love without any conditions or hidden beliefs of what someone needs to do, according to your belief system. Our beliefs can do a lot of damage to others as we restrict their spiritual growth by wanting them to be like us.

> Recipe for success: keep it simple! Connect to the Light of God, smile, and send love.

2

How Does Distance Healing Work?

Distance healing is real! It really works! Never underestimate the power of prayer frequencies. With distance healing you are tapping into the Divine Frequencies of the Universe that are high vibrational and have their own intelligence. I never considered that a vibration had intelligence or thought it rational until I started to understand how distance healing worked. The intelligence within the Light is what makes it possible for anyone to do distance healing. You don't need a college education to work with the intelligence; you just need a willingness to align to a power greater than your own. You are plugging into a light source that has many frequencies within the Matrix.

When we initiate a distance healing we are joined to the other person by strings and strands of Light that mesh into one Light, the Universal God Light. If our Light isn't the highest standard of healing light, our connection will not be as effective and will fall short of the correct vibration needed for healing. Did you know you can advertise on the inner planes with your Light? I do it all the time and it's very effective and costs nothing except my time.

TIME TO JOURNEY INTO THE FIELD/THE MATRIX

When doing distance healing we work in a Matrix, a Field: a medium that connects two or more points in space, usually via a force like gravity or electromagnetism. In the Matrix is a sea of quantum fields connecting *everything*. When we do distance healing we are working in this sea of Quantum Fields. That's what makes distance healing easy and understandable. Everyone has a Light signature, a frequency imprint just like a fingerprint; we can dial them up by saying their name. Yes, it's that easy and the more we know them the easier it is to make a connection and if we sleep with them we are never disconnected, no matter how far apart we are at any given time. That's why it's easy to tell what our significant other is really thinking. Scary, huh!

HOW WE INTERPRET THE FIELD

I also found that the body holds thought forms around it like icons on the computer. Whatever is in our consciousness shows up in our auric field as a vibrational picture. Others around us interpret our Field with their Field as we mix at work and play, and if they have like pictures we will be drawn to them, usually for a lesson of some kind.

Seeing into the field of an individual while working in person was the forerunner to seeing over a great distance when correcting Light patterns in someone's field. I found that using the telephone was an additional assist when looking at someone's Field. There seemed to be a clearer picture of them when talking on the phone. It happened gradually with each encounter of the Light of someone, when they were somewhere else. I found it most fascinating how easy it was to click and drag the hologram of the person I was talking with to a blank wall to observe where their Light frequency was skewed. Usually all it took to correct the Light was relaying what I observed. As the healer, we have to believe that it's possible and allow all possibilities to happen. It's almost as simple as someone telling us there is dirt on the back of our pants. We will want to remove the dirt, correct? When I observe Light in the Field of an individual I am not correcting the Light I am only relaying what I observe. The Higher Consciousness of the individual makes the changes once it becomes obvious, not me. Remember you're not there to heal them; you're there for the healing to take place.

INSTANT QUANTUM SHIFTING

I first noticed the instant quantum shift in the Field of someone while working at a metaphysical bookstore in Nashville, Tennessee giving Angel readings. Many spirits are around us at all times and they become visible while working at the Zero Point Level (this is an altered state of consciousness). During each reading I would ask for guidance and for a clear connection to any and all angelic influences associated with whomever I was speaking. As I made each connection into their Field, colored Light would become visible around them. When the Light was muddy or dark I knew the frequency was not what it should be for their good health. When I relayed to them what I had seen, the energy would clear and later their pain in that area would be gone. I knew that I had not done anything significant to allow a healing to take place, so what just happened? I didn't touch them; I had not said any kind of prayer for healing; I hadn't even asked for a healing, it just happened without my consent! Evidently God didn't need my input to make it happen. Back then I didn't understand I was at Zero Point Energy, but I did realize after much contemplation that I was connecting to the highest aspect of the individual; the Higher Self was doing the correcting. I have found that until we become aware of some infraction with our health we are not going to do anything about it. In quantum physics there is no equation for the observer; it's only what the observer sees. Remember you're not there to heal them; you're there for the healing to take place.

WHY NOT USE THE TELEPHONE?

Now that you know everything is connected to something else, doesn't that make it easier to understand how distance healing works? Have you ever considered using the light already in place with a phone call as your medium for practicing distance healing? The phone seems to enhance the healing session. I don't know how it works; I just know that it does. I can't tell you how my smartphone works, but I know it does because I can hear the other person talking. That alone seems like a miracle to me. I love modern science with all the gadgets and tools available for us to use in creative ways.

THE PHONE IS MAGICAL! IT'S REALLY BIG!

Just like the iPhone is science at work, so is distance healing. All we need is the vibrational frequency of whomever we are connecting; their vibrational code is their phone number to the inner planes. When someone would call and make an appointment for a session to restore their Light I would talk with them for awhile on the phone to see what was going on in their world. While talking I found that I could see things in a holographic format. It looks a lot like the negatives we used to have when taking pictures, long before digital cameras came into use.

You can move into another realm very easily on the phone because your connection is already established by the call. I have reasoned this must be the established Light made possible by the phone call that carries the individual's voice in a matrix kind of venue. (I'm sure AT&T would charge extra if they only knew, so don't tell them.) Your Ether Tube is already in place by the phone call, which is very handy. Another good thing about the phone is that it's easier dealing with someone's personality and story than in person.

> It's just easier to do distance healing when you know how to use all the Divine Principles of the universe.

HOW I PREPARE FOR A PHONE SESSION?

I get centered ("Be still and know that I am God" kind of moment) and connect my Light to the edges of the Universe and beyond and into my earth chakra. I want to feel balanced and in the flow of God Light. "As above, so below." I hold this a few minutes and smile while connecting to the Light. I smile while doing any kind of work in the Light; it keeps you plugged into a Higher God Frequency. I think that alone is a very cool thing to know and practice.

Once I feel balanced and connected I have a short interview with the caller. While conversing, I try to avoid giving the unbalanced frequency of the caller too much power by focusing on every symptom. Whatever we focus on is where we put our attention. If our focus is on cancer, colds and flu, we are creating more cancer, colds and flu. All I want them to realize is there is an off-frequency that needs to be reconnected to a higher vibrational Light. When you get too much information your focus may be fractured into too many avenues of belief. We will start believing that the cancer has power over us or the cold and flu has more power than the Light it takes for a healing. Keep it simple by giving them the power to self-heal as you hold the space for them to transform their vibration. Let them know that their frequency is changing as you see the Light change colors to a more beneficial flow of God Light. It isn't necessary for you to see the Light for the change to take place. However, it is necessary for you to believe that it's possible and to know that the Light has changed by your ability to believe. Remember, when you gaze on a quantum particle it changes by the act of observation and if the consciousness that is observing has the correct belief system in place, miracles happen.

We will get to know what information is not necessary when working in the Quantum Field. We don't have to know everything to assist someone's energy in bringing that person into a higher vibrational Light. In a quantum environment we will be in a place where all things exist at the same time and all things are possible. Whatever we want to call it, we are in the Zone! Magic can happen, which gives that person a new sense of well-being to move forward in life.

Remember when working in the Quantum Field, all you need is the architect's drawing, not the finished house. Allow the Light of God to construct the vision being held by the observer; making sure the observer can hold the vision.

Light has consciousness and we can speak to the Light in its own language. It's more of a frequency-based language, a knowing that we are a part of whatever is taking place in the Light at any given moment. I know this sounds confusing, but really it isn't, once we learn the divine principles of working in the Universal Light of God. We converse with the Light by acknowledging that a Higher Power is present and that the Higher Power knows what needs to transpire. We allow the Light to be its perfect Self without any instructions or judgments. The intelligence in the Light will do the healing. We are to believe that a healing is possible and give thanks for the healing that has already happened due to our belief.

HIVE MENTALITY

Suffering exists only because we become attached to a particular form or belief. We have to let go and remove all resistance to changing the vibration. We have become like the Borg on Star Trek; their belief statement is "Resistance is futile, you will be assimilated." We belong to the collective unconscious, which is like the Borg to a certain degree, and it will own us, until it doesn't! Whatever is in the group consciousness of our town, our state, and our home will be what we vibrate to, until we don't. The *don't* part comes by allowing new creative thought patterns that are in opposition to many people around us that have no desire to listen to our beliefs. For the most part, they will push us away telling us that we have changed. Ninety percent of the time if we stay true to our new beliefs, old friends will come back into our life. When I stepped onto the spiritual path many of my friends thought I had lost my mind and tried hard to get me to return to their standard belief of what "THEY" thought was best for me. I remained true to my journey and after a while they wanted back in my life after they had accepted me as I was.

HEALING THROUGH A SURROGATE

I have clients call from other states and we work on whatever is going on in their field while on the phone. I like to think of it as adjusting the Light frequency to its perfect harmonic vibration. I find that it's best not to focus on the malady and only concentrate on the Light Quotient that is being adjusted.

Going through a surrogate has been very effective, allowing me to see them clearer by using the established Light of the caller. While talking on the phone with someone we have the grand opportunity to slip into their Quantum Field easily. If the caller needs assistance with family members we can use the caller as a surrogate to access the Light of their loved ones. We have previously put the caller into a tube of Light as we worked with them, so it isn't necessary to put them in another tube of Light unless we want to. We can't overdo using the Light. My next step is to ask permission to go through their heart and soul to the heart and soul of whomever we are connecting with. This is attaching to their Light through the Field by speaking the necessary code, which is their name. We then place the loved one in a tube of Light and proceed to correct whatever is amiss in their hologram. Ninety-nine percent of the time callers already have a strong Light connection established with whomever they are concerned about. This simple process gives access to their

Light signatures even though we are not speaking directly to them. Mostly when we are using the caller as a surrogate it's about a family member, and trust me: there are many strands of Light already attached to each individual, especially if it's a mom calling about her child. The energy of a mom owns the child even after she is long gone and only a memory. I know you didn't want to hear that, but it's true!

After each session of working in the caller's Field through distance healing, the caller can always tell a difference with themselves and everyone that was readjusted in the Light.

ADJUSTING THEIR HOLOGRAM

You have to love Quantum Physics; when you look at a particle of light, it changes just because it's being observed. The process is looking at their hologram, acknowledging what is being shown in the hologram and observing the changes in their Quantum Field of Light through the observation. However, the Light is affected by the consciousness of the one doing the observing, so I have to believe that it's possible for the Light that I'm observing to God-correct on its own. I never say, "God, heal Javed, my grandson of his horrible cold." I just recognize where Javed's Light is not correct and allow the Light to adjust to its perfect God-vibration. The more I can stay out of the way of the energy that is flowing, the faster God can reset my grandson's Light.

THE FAMILY ENTITY INFLUENCE

We are all connected, but those we live with or the ones that gave us birth are strongly interwoven into our Field. It doesn't matter if Mom has been dead for years; you still have a strong connection to every tread of Light she created on planet Earth. That's all part of the family entity. "Part of the what?" you ask. Yes, we create an entity with all our family beliefs wrapped up in a nice little package that for the most part can't be tampered with. It becomes a living, breathing thing that requires our complete dedication to the family beliefs, which we are obligated to by birth into the family line. The family entity becomes so strong in some families we could dress it and give it a seat at the Sunday dinner table. It's loyalty to the tribe above all else and the tribe is more than one generation with which you must deal.

Is that not the weirdest thing you have ever heard? Yes, it is; and the bad part is its true and will control us until you step up and say, "You people are crazy and I don't believe the same as you believe anymore. I love you, but I'm not going to bow to the family entity any longer. I've found a new directive that I have hitched my wagon to and will be on my way." Now we become the odd man out in the family and will have to deal again with energies beyond our control until the family entity realizes we are not going to change and allows us to be ourselves. It all comes from our knowing who we are and being willing to be different from everyone else in our family line. We have to laugh about the things in life that we can't change and we have to find a common ground or a way to deal with the obstacle. We might as well give into the process of what is going on around us and the family. If we resist, it will persist and dig some deep claws into our Soul.

UNDERSTANDING THE FAMILY ENTITY: STRINGS AND STRANDS OF THE FAMILY

Your birthright comes with eyes like Dad's, smile like Mom's and a build like Grandpa's. Our height is sometimes regulated by our family line; our skin color is influenced by our family line; the languages we speak come from the territory where we were born. Did you know that we inherit more than these traits I have mentioned? We also receive at birth the streams of energy that run through the family line and if *crazy* is deeply embedded, we will be imbued with that trait or predisposed to bringing it to the surface.

We had lots of growth in our family tree that needed to be pruned with a machete, so I know what I'm talking about. You may feel the same way as you think about some of the members of your family tree. The roots will keep growing in our world until we decide to shift into another conscious way of thinking. We can become the catalyst for changing the frequencies of our entire family line by changing our beliefs. Our focus is not changing the beliefs of the entire family; we just hold steady with our new truths. When we can hold a new truth in place it will vibrate through all quantum states of the family line, sending a shock wave down the family tree. It's like magic, but its Spiritual Technology doing the work for us as our family phases back into their Divine Heritage and the frequency of *crazy* disappears from family gatherings.

I started working with family entities around 1999 while assisting clients in clearing their family lines before going home for the holidays. They dreaded the prospect of experiencing the family for a week, knowing that the same insanity would have to be dealt with once again. Memories of childhood humiliation and injustice would not go away and clung to them like a wet shirt, as it crept into their conscious reality. They would rather be covered in honey and tied to an ant hill in the noonday sun than go home for the holidays.

When they returned from their visit after being cleared, they would call and excitedly tell me how wonderful the visit was and how well everyone got along and that it was the best holiday ever. Now remember, we only cleared the family line from the client's energy base and it cleared everyone else. How God is that?

I had a woman come for a clearing concerning her family and how they chided her every time they got together for the number of unsuccessful relationships she'd had over the years. Each experience would take on a life of its own while she was with them, making her miserable and unable to enjoy the visit. We cleared her of each part she played dealing with relationships from her past. Since she had suffered post-traumatic stress from the other family gatherings, she was blown away when no one mentioned anything to her about her being a loser in the love department the next time they gathered. She said one person started to say something and stopped in mid-sentence, and it was surreal as she observed everyone from a more detached perspective. I asked her if she truly understood what happened? She admitted that she only had a vague idea of what happened at the family gathering. She said, "I understand the results, but not perfectly clear on how we got them."

GETTING RESULTS

She did admit she understood that forgiveness helped. What she didn't understand was the Spiritual Technology at work. When she revealed her past beliefs concerning relationships in her life, we looked at the truths she made. When she found the truths, she could then reveal them as a barefaced lie. The next step involved forgiving herself and other perpetrators in each event. Willingly cutting the ties and freeing the other participants to go their own ways allowed her actual truth to surface. The last step was telling them, "I love you as a God-being, but I am no longer willing to take responsibility for your actions. You are free to go whatever direction you choose. I am no longer in charge of your Light connections. Time to say, Thank you, God."

Think about it: Those family members she forgave were not in the room with her; they were miles away. They never heard a word she said about forgiving them and they were affected. Her vibrational energy of Love and forgiveness traveled all over middle Tennessee making the necessary changes as she sat in my kitchen, sipping her tea. You have to admit that's pretty phenomenal. Distance and time doesn't matter when sending healing love down the family line.

Unless we are willing to see our world as it truly is we will never evolve into the people we are meant to be. Let's keep a bottle of God-strength window cleaner handy to polish the windows of our Soul, thus revealing our world clearly through the polished surface every day. Smile! We have just committed Spiritual Technology.

NORMALIZING UN-TRUTHS IN OUR LIVES

We have already talked about the family entity and how we are owned to a certain extent by this frequency running amuck through our family line. Now let's talk about how we take the lies we hear and see, making them our truth by normalizing the illusion.

We become imprinted when we normalize things, such as seeing Mom and Dad with glasses; we normalize that we must have glasses also. Look around at families and see how many are wearing glasses if Mom and Dad wear glasses. Most everyone in my family wore glasses and had bifocals by the time they were forty. I thought Granny's half-inch-thick glasses were the ugliest things I had ever seen and I didn't want to wear ugly bifocals. I was nearsighted and needed glasses by fifth grade, but I still don't have bifocals. I know it had something to do with me making a conscious decision to never wear those ugly things. Divine Consciousness is an equal opportunity state-of-mind.

We have normalized aging to the point that we expect to start showing our age by the time we are fifty; parents and grandparents are showing wrinkles and slowing down. We see the evidence before us and normalize it; but when the truth is known, we don't have to age like everyone else. Our bodies are designed to last much longer than they do, but the evidence is there before us every day as we look at Mom/Dad, Grandma/Grandpa and the mirror, so we make it normal for us to get old like them. It's tough to pull away from what you consider normal and embrace Supernatural Living, but we can do it with a little faith in ourselves.

I wasn't aware of the aging illusion until I was already fifty. Darn! I wish I had known about this a few decades earlier. Oh, well! I know now that I don't have to age like everyone around me, so I am working with my consciousness to plug into the new belief; I can live a lot longer than statistics reveal. In fact, I want to live long enough for people to ask the question, is that crusty old broad ever going to die?

We have to be very careful about family disease also, for we will vibrate to the frequency of our loved ones. This is not an intentional thing, it just happens as we get caught up in the flow of the energies. We don't realize we have just flipped the switch to become something we didn't really intend. I have seen families where cancer takes hold of the whole family. My sister, for instance, has a great fear of developing colon cancer like our dad. I don't have it in my consciousness to bring this to me and it's hard for me to understand her unnatural fear about something that probably won't happen. I explained to her that it's not necessary to have colon cancer; she doesn't have the same lifestyle or eat the same rich foods as our Dad did. We can absorb the wrong belief frequency like a sponge soaks up spilled water.

I know a couple where the husband was on a breathing machine and the wife ended up on a breathing machine a few years later. He had shoulder surgery and she had shoulder surgery some time later. He has diabetes and now she has diabetes. I know some of this is from their lifestyle, but some of it is from normalizing what is in their thought processes as they think, "This will probably happen to me."

Family idiosyncrasies are some of the funniest things we have normalized. What is normal to one family is ludicrous to another. Have you noticed interactions of a family coming together as a unit, whether it's at a restaurant or the park? Each family "acts out" their own absurdities as they interact. Your family might laugh out loud when seeing another family all dressed in the same matching outfits, while the matching family may think your family doesn't care enough to make everyone look similar. We normalize lots of activities: how we hold a fork when we eat, because that's the way Dad held his fork; elbows on the table because that's what everyone does when we're at the table. Maybe it will be the style of clothing we wear because that's the way our family has always dressed. We have to be stylish; or an iron never touches our clothing! We normalize the rules of card games according to who taught us to play, though there are many ways to play.

We normalize bad attitudes, blaming it on being tired or having a bad time with work and responsibilities. We normalize lewd behavior because we see Dad's lewd behavior and if Dad does it, we can also. We normalize the language of the family because we hear bad grammar and inappropriate language every day in the home, so this must be an acceptable way to speak as we talk to others. It's the same as if we were born in France; there we would speak French and have a French accent. We become the vibration that's around us every day in our normalized life.

The Field mirrors now, not the future, not the past, so what we choose to experience in the present must feel in our hearts like it has already happened. If we keep saying it will happen someday, the Field will keep reflecting "someday."

GIVING PERMISSION FOR AN ENERGY TO GO TO WORK

It's not that we need to *get* permission for an energy to go to work as much as *give* permission for an energy to go to work. There is always a Divine Directive present anytime we facilitate a healing. The intelligence within any energetic action of Light must be acknowledged for successful transference of healing frequencies.

WHAT DO YOU MEAN BY THAT?

Giving permission means we have to surrender our judgment of the outcome of the healing. What we believe about healing is nowhere close to what healing is about. Sure we can move a little energy, make someone feel better or relaxed, but is that all we want to do? We may even see an improvement in their condition to some extent. Is that enough? Why not assist them in creating their healing? Our job is to be present, holding the perfect image of a healing, allowing the healing to take place.

To be effective with distance healing we need to be willing to let go of everything we have been taught about healing. The known rules we have obligated ourselves to seem to be lukewarm at best. We have to unplug every circuit we have plugged into a belief about healing and allow our Light to connect to the highest level of our Divine Principle.

IF WE CAN SEE IT, WE CAN DO SOMETHING ABOUT IT!

Whatever we are allowed to see in another's energy Field, we have a connection to in the Field. We have the ability to connect to the intelligence of these connections and clear what is present just by observing. The person who's Field we are observing need not participate except to hear what we see. His or her Higher Self/Soul Level Self will react to what we see and it will self-correct. I know this sounds like an Obi-Wan Kenobi thing, but it isn't. It's just the applied science of working in the Field of Spiritual Technology. It seems like magic and miracles, but it's just science at work doing a spiritual thing.

SEEING THEM AS A HOLOGRAM WHILE IN A TUBE OF LIGHT

We are in an altered state while viewing the holograms of others; working with our unconscious mind to tap into other realms. Our conscious mind will not be of much assistance, so phase out of that state as quickly as possible. After you do this a few times you will slip into an altered state just by saying, "I need to look at their hologram."

When I first started seeing the holograms of individuals as I spoke with them on the phone, it seemed like a pretty natural thing to be doing. I had just asked to see their Light images and would scan the images to see what was off in their Fields. The more I looked at individuals this way the easier it was to communicate with their Field. I found that whatever I could see in their holograms could be changed with little effort. It was like their body elemental was showing me what to do. Mostly all I did was make the person on the phone aware of what was out of alignment and usually it self-corrected when they received the information. If we know something is off we will correct it, but if we don't have a clue, we won't do anything because we can't see past the pain and suffering. Distance healing is such a unique experience because we are working in the Quantum Field and when we see their hologram we are at Zero Point Energy (the state of all possibilities): the place where miracles happen. (It seems like miracles, but it's just applied science at work.)

This is an advanced technique that we can achieve and utilize in our work. It takes practice and belief in ourselves; plus, we have to go to those unknown territories in our brain and create a new link to our conscious awareness. It's more midbrain and associated with our "third eye." This is not hard to achieve or beyond our ability; it's just a different way of getting somewhere. It's doing something different than we usually do. We all have the same mind centers available for us to activate and utilize; we just need to be aware of their existence and having a little knowledge of how to connect speeds the process. Don't allow untruths to cause second-guessing of your abilities.

When we have placed someone in the Reiki symbol *Hon Sha Ze Sho Nen*, it's like hermetically sealing the person in a chamber impervious to outside influence. The *Hon Sha Ze Sho Nen* forms an ether tube that holds the integrity of the Light being used. This is a good thing, especially if we are viewing the person's body as a hologram. When viewing as a hologram we can request the hologram to turn and see all sides, which is pretty cool. We are not told we can do these kinds of things, so we don't. I tell you it's available to everyone! Every time I tell a student you can do this, that they have everything within them to complete the task, they do it!

I don't tell them until afterwards how extraordinary they are to see anyone in a holographic format. Many things are possible for us to achieve if we only have awareness of the possibility.

HOW TO VIEW THE BODY OF SOMEONE IN A HOLOGRAPHIC FORMAT

Until people have a flicker of comprehension that something is possible they will tell us it's not possible because no one they know has ever done it before and will stamp it with some kind of label. Something like, "You are crazy and out of your mind if you think I am going to invest a single brain cell in storing this information." Most people have to hear it over and over again before it begins to get their attention. We already have enough of our own unconscious counter beliefs affecting us to allow more negative thoughts to infiltrate our consciousness; we can't allow the naysayers to direct our life. When you get to the place where you can stand your own ground concerning your beliefs, encounters with unbelievers crossing your path will happen less and less. My Mantra is: "I know who I am and am free to be me." There is freedom in knowing who you are and being able to be yourself at all times.

To see someone's hologram you have to go somewhere else in your mind. I know, you are saying, "What is she talking about?" Until we realize we have other programs available in our unconscious, we will never be able to complete the task of seeing on the inner planes. We don't have to understand how the programs work in order to make them work. We have to believe they are present and that we can learn this new Spiritual Technology. Once your belief is in place you can get to work by asking to see someone as a hologram. Once you ask to see someone's hologram, take a deep breath and relax, allowing your relaxed mind to shift you into another state of consciousness. Once you are in the Alpha meditative state you can practice the Spiritual Technology of seeing on the inner planes of someone. This is something you have to do more than once to achieve success.

While viewing someone on the telephone we already have an established Light. Once we have made the connection on the phone we are instantly in a place to start seeing. Now we need to bring our consciousness on board with us. We reach this space easily by acknowledging the possibility. Take a couple of deep breaths and go somewhere else in your mind. Because we know and believe it's easy to connect to our third eye, our third eye will be most accommodating. We have to acknowledge that it's possible for us to work in this venue. If we do not respect the intelligence of our unconsciousness, our unconsciousness will not reveal anything to us. Our belief is part of the code to get us to the place of seeing what we need to see.

Asking to see may not give us access the first time we ask. When I started working with Sonora I found it difficult to see anything the first few times she worked with me. But eventually, it took only one glimpse into the inner planes to start laying down the necessary pathways of neural networks. When this happens nothing can stop you from moving forward. We now have something to reason with, when before we only had a hypothesis. Once our conscious brain has someplace to attach, we can move forward quickly. This only comes from being consistent in our approach to mastering the ability.

This technique also assists us in remote viewing. I have looked at my house after driving a few miles down the road to see if I left the lights on in the house or maybe the stove on. It's a very handy technique to have. When traveling around town I can look ahead at the traffic and see if I need to take a different route. This has helped countless times. Before you laugh and shake your head, give it a try. What do you have to lose? Nothing but a little time.

> Awareness and Presence always happens now. If you are trying to make something happen you are creating resistance to what is. Removing all resistance allows evolutionary energy to unfold. Eckert Tolle

3

Can Anyone Be
A Healer?

All that is required to be a successful healer is a willing spirit with the ability to love. If being pure of thought and a clear of mind were required, I would have a few burn marks from lightning bolts being hurled in my direction. I have pushed the envelope more than once with God and I am still alive to talk about it, so don't be concerned about being a saint. Practicing distance healing does not require sainthood.

WHERE SHOULD THE THOUGHTS OF THE HEALER RESIDE?

When we look at something with our mind we are looking at the consciousness of the thought. We become the thought by the act of observing and whatever we are observing changes because we have given it our consciousness. As the theologian Søren Kierkegaard said, "If you name me, you negate me by giving me a name, a label; you negate all the other things I could possibly be." You lock the particles into being a thing, by pinning it down and naming it. But at the same time, you are creating it; you are defining it to exist. We have taken on the responsibility of our creation.

We are responsible for what appears in our world, because we are the Divine creators of what exists and this is defined by our ability to see our creation. I just could not believe that I had any part in creating all the crazy attitudes and bad judgments of people around me. I knew that I had no part in the way they looked at life and I certainly didn't deserve being held accountable for their actions toward me--it wasn't my fault! Does this sound familiar? It should! We all react the same way to new thoughts and ideas. We keep asking the wrong questions and not getting the correct answers.

When we come to the place of changing the questions we may start to receive answers. Instead of asking, "Why did they do that to me?" ask, "What part did I play in being the butt-end of their joke?" What did I contribute energetically that plugged me into the low vibrational Light frequency of nasty people? What prevented me from seeing the lie? Our programs that run continuously distort our vision. We end up looking through the dirty windows of our Soul and only see what our consciousness allows us to see.

ACCEPTING DIFFERENT THOUGHT

Søren Kierkegaard made his quotation in 1855 long before anyone had ever heard of Zero point energy. He already understood the Schrodinger equation, which states, "there is a wave associated with any particle (like the electron), and it is called the wave function and it is spread out to fill the whole universe. " But there is a catch, and a weird, very weird one: when we look at an electron or measure it with a particle detector, the wave function is said to collapse.

The act of observation has included us in the consciousness of the particles we are measuring (observing) and everything becomes part of our consciousness, because we have become aware of its existence.

We are the creator of everything in our lives as we observe and make judgments; we are measuring with our own particle detectors and creating what is present within our thoughts at that moment in time. Our thoughts are more powerful than we ever imagined. We swim daily in the sea of Quantum Fields that surround us; being a part of everything and everyone on the planet. Time as we know it is only an illusion; we are a part of everything in the past, present and future at the same time. It only becomes apparent when we lock the particles in place by our observation.

I JUST DID WHAT?

How wonderfully frightening is that thought? It's wonderful to think that we can change the particles around us by observing them, but at the same time we lock the particles in place with our judgments of what we see according to our beliefs. What if our beliefs are limiting at the moment of observation? What if we are in the act of condemning others' actions; are we creating more of their actions? How much responsibility do we take for what is showing up in our world? Once this new reality shows up through our observing everything around us we have the opportunity to change the construct we have created by our observations. This repeats itself over and over in our lives. Can you think of a time when the same scenario kept replaying over and over in your life?

We can use the same principle in life as we struggle to make circumstances change in the people we love. Instead of praying for them to stop taking drugs, drinking, smoking, or other irresponsible behaviors, start seeing them as a perfect "God Being" in the moment. If we can't see it, they definitely can't see it. If we can't get past the personality of the one we love, we will never see a change. When having trouble seeing God in the person who is passed out on the sofa and reeking of alcohol, see him as a baby while you send your unconditional love.

DO NOT INCLUDE REQUIREMENTS IN YOUR PRAYERS

Don't deny you have never been guilty of making deals with God or giving instruction to the person receiving your prayers. We all have guilty faces on this one.

Prayer example 1: God, I come to you in prayer for Joey, the good-for-nothing boyfriend of mine. God, he needs to change his wicked ways and stop drinking and running around and get a steady job.

Prayer example 2: God, you know I talked to you about Shirley yesterday and the day before and I can't see any change in that woman. Are you sure you are listening to me? She is still hateful to everyone at work.

Prayer example 3: God, what are you going to do about little Samuel? He is still not paying attention to his mother and God you know how I try with that boy. I have been praying for him all his life and this is the thanks I get.

PRAYER SOLUTIONS

Have you ever prayed a prayer like these prayers? I have in the past as I talked to God with my best self-righteous intentions. I knew what was best for them and I was going to pray them into submission! I will say that the people I religiously prayed for didn't change by my prayers and all it did was put a deeper gap between us. I just figured God was busy with other sinners and would get around to taking care of my requests sooner or later.

To be effective in our prayers all we should be doing is realizing God: that we have that holy place within where the presence of God is always available. Holding fast to the truth of the ever-presence of God in our lives is essential to being a healer. Nothing exists that isn't God-infused and we are Divine principals of God. When we pray, we pray that the love of God move through us to whatever

55

circumstance. We don't pray for the circumstance to be healed; if we were to do that we would be coming from a place of separation from God. The truth is, it's already healed waiting for us to align to the healing that is present. There is never a time that God isn't present in our lives. So all we have to do is thank God for the healing and be in agreement with the healing and smile. Remember you're not there to heal them; you're there for the healing to take place.

As healers we have the responsibility to believe that God is always present in every circumstance and that whatever is appearing is only illusion. We are mesmerized by our programs of belief, which we must override for truth to appear. Truth is realizing the necessity to believe our Oneness and that there is no separation. We must let go of the dogma; the results of other people's thinking and move out of the hive mentality. We have all been assimilated too long into everyone else's beliefs. We are our own people and hold the responsibility to formulate our own truths and to let go of the beliefs of family, society, and friends. We have to change, "it is futile to resist" into "I can do whatever I please with my life and you can't stop me from embracing the freedom of thought."

CAUSE AND EFFECT

From <u>The Thunder of Silence</u> by Joel Goldsmith

"Resist not evil" sounds like the most foolish and impractical of human teachings, yet it is the wisest and most practical of spiritual principles. Those who attain a state of consciousness in which they can let the energy come to them with the armor of the world—with spears, knives, guns, or lawsuit—and can stand in complete confidence with no resistance, can never lose.....

As long as we resist evil, we are not living under Grace but under the law: and the very knife that we throw at another will boomerang to pierce us in the chest, all in a blinding flash and out of nowhere. There is no way for Grace to descend upon us if we are indulging the human way of life.....

The Master reveals the basic karmic law of as ye sow, so shall ye reap, but he also makes plain the one sure and certain way to rise above the law of cause and effect, and that is not to set in motion a cause—to do nothing, think nothing, and be nothing of ourselves. For example, if we pray with some object or purpose in mind, we are likely to produce an effect in accordance with the cause which we set up. But if we were to pray without an object, solely for the realization of God, then we would not have set up a cause, and there could be no effect. There would only be God Itself appearing as the harmony of our existence.

.....When we relinquish the thoughts and things of this world and live in a continuous desire to know God aright, leaving all other considerations aside, and then when God is realized, God appears in our experience as a perfected life....

There are countless books authored by Joel that give us something tangible to hold onto when things are slippery in our life. I feel blessed that his works found a way into my library and my heart. If you need bricks to create the path you travel in this lifetime, I suggest you start reading books by enlightened authors like Joel Goldsmith.

"Once you make a decision, the universe conspires to make it happen." - Ralph Waldo Emerson

THE SOUL

The Soul is affectionately connected to the heart and the heart is affectionately connected to the subconscious. A necessary congruency is bonded between the two when we are open to our spiritual evolution as we become aware of our oneness. New centers of awareness are expanded in our consciousness making it possible for us to connect on a spiritual level to the Divine within. We become self-realized knowing that God is within every cell of our physical aspect.

It's easy to comprehend that the Soul is working through our unconsciousness. What's not so easy to understand is what the Soul is actually doing. As I have said before, the Soul is affectionately connected to the heart and the heart is ruled by the subconscious. Having this information gives us a clue as to why we point our finger at someone else for what is playing out in our world. It's essential that we stop and ask that hard-to-access part of us, "What is going on here?" If we know it's our responsibility to ask, then we are more apt to strike up a conversation with our subconscious connection. That's when we finally understand that if we don't ask we will never get any logical answers as to why things happen. Just ask your question expecting an answer. Sometimes I demand an answer; that's why I know God is unoffendable.

I remember a time when I was just learning the spiritual principles of life, trying to understand the repetitive circumstances playing out in my life. I would sit and often ask, "Why God? Why does the same thing keep happening over and over?" After bellyaching for way too long, I told God in a loud voice that I was through with this insanity happening in my life and I wasn't going to put up with it happening any longer. There you go, God! I am no longer willing to take the crap the universe is hurling my way! I have learned everything I need to learn from this situation and I have the T-shirt to prove it! It's a done deal as far as I am concerned.

The results? No lightning bolts were hurled in my direction, so I exhaled and sat quietly for a few minutes. From somewhere within I heard a voice say, "That is well and good and you don't have to experience that again. All that was required is your realization that you have learned what you need to learn from the situation. I got so upset when I heard this that I stayed mad at God for about two weeks. I kept saying over and over, out loud, "You mean all I had to say was, I got it! I have learned what needed to be learned and ready to move on and I don't have to experience this again?" The voice said, "Yes." I moaned and groaned, fussing at God for days until finally I sat down and laughed a good laugh, knowing the power of God's love had seeped through the barnacles of my beliefs and made me a better person. I look back now and smile at this up-close and personal encounter with my Soul.

You have to understand my mind never shuts down and it moves faster than a 57 Chevy in a drag race. Once I believe I have learned something, it's hard to change that belief. Be open and in agreement to every message that comes to you. It may not be a voice; it may be a knowing when you awaken the next morning. If you earnestly ask for an answer, you will receive one every time. I always do when I have my, "Be still and know that I am God Moments." Quite your mind and a clear message will come to your conscious mind.

I'm telling you these things to make it easier for you to interpret the difference between real and illusion. Every time I arrive at the mistaken conclusion that I know the facts, I am shown that I don't know diddly-squat. If you think you are aware of everything in your world, you could possibly be in for a surprise without the delights included. The following article will assist in proving how we don't see the obvious when we are so focused on the task at hand.

INVISIBLE GORILLA TEST

To test for inattentional blindness, researchers ask participants to complete a primary task while an unexpected stimulus is presented. Afterwards, researchers ask participants if they saw anything unusual during the primary task. The best-known study demonstrating inattentional blindness is the Invisible gorilla test, conducted by Daniel Simons of the University of Illinois at Urbana-Champaign and Christopher Chabris of Harvard University. This study, a revised version of earlier studies conducted by Ulric Neisser, Neisser and Becklen, 1975, asked subjects to watch a short video of two groups of people (wearing black and white t-shirts) pass a basketball around. The subjects are told to either count the number of passes made by one of the teams or to keep count of bounce passes vs. aerial passes. In different versions of the video a woman walks through the scene carrying an umbrella, or wearing a full gorilla suit. After watching the video the subjects are asked if they saw anything out of the ordinary take place. In most groups, 50% of the subjects did not report seeing the lady with the umbrella or the gorilla. The failure to perceive the gorilla or the woman carrying an umbrella is attributed to the failure to attend to it while engaged in the difficult task of counting the number of passes of the ball. These results indicate that the relationship between what is in one's visual field and perception is based much more on attention than was previously thought. Very interesting! The invisible Gorilla.com

We have forgotten that it's innate for us to be our own healers. Everyone has the capacity and the equipment to heal; it's their free will choice in life. Let go of any preconceived notions that you don't have the ability to heal. You just need to be reminded that you have a God-Self that is always – all the time – present. When we reach this state of comprehension we understand our oneness and our Divinity as we embrace Spiritual Technology, producing a supernatural lifestyle.

Question Number

4

What Does Quantum Physics Have To Do With Distance Healing?

YOU HAVE TO BE REWIRED

When we focus on the belief of cancer, heart trouble, warts or whatever may be appearing as reality before us, we create more of what is our focus. When we focus on the Light of the individual we can refine the Light without being inside the condition that is present. This job is done in the Quantum Field and the Quantum Field is the medium we must make friends with and acknowledge its existence. "There is intelligence within the Field." The more we acknowledge the intelligence in the Field, the more markers we put in place producing a stronger Light connection through our dedicated application of thought. Once established, pebbles we dropped along the way will remain in place, giving us easy access over and over to time-space travel.

It's just applied science. It's not some sort of hocus-pocus magic or miracles; it's just the rules of the Universe being obeyed. I'm not talking Newtonian science; I'm talking about the science of Spiritual Technology. Scoot over and allow new thought to squeeze itself onto your park bench. When we have only a mustard seed of belief, we can change the world around us.

When we understand the quantum aspect of our existence and that there is more to our world than is visible to the naked eye, we can better comprehend reality. A paradigm shift must occur in the consciousness. Rewiring occurs when old thought programs are seen with new eyes as we freely let go of the known and embrace the unknown; when the truth we have paid homage to for years reveals itself as folly. That's when we connect to an intelligence within that was unknown before. We are achieving spiritual alchemy as we explore the technology of quantum reality.

WHAT ARE YOU TRYING TO TELL ME?

Now you're telling me that I'm possessed and there is a part of me that has its own intelligence and I don't even know it? No, I am telling you there is more to our consciousness than we may be aware of at this time. We know about our conscious mind; we have conversations with it all the time. We all have some concept of our subconscious mind, but do we truly know how the conscious mind and the subconscious mind communicate? Do we know about our higher aspect, called your Higher Consciousness/Super-Consciousness (the really smart part of us)? We never talk to it; why? Mainly because we don't even know it is possible to speak to this highest aspect of ourselves.

How do we communicate with a part of our consciousness that has all the answers to every question we have ever asked; that knows everything we could possibly need to know to live a full and happy existence on planet Earth? We must learn the language of the subconscious to get in the door. The one big fly in the ointment is that we have to go through the subconscious to access the Superconscious. Just think about it. We don't even know how to converse with the subconscious and it rules our life. To get to the highest aspect we have to let go and downsize our beliefs. We try to do the carry-on luggage thing, trying to stuff a few more beliefs inside and still zip our suitcase. The airlines realize carrying all that extra unnecessary weight takes more fuel to fly the plane. That's why they have started charging for the bags we check and have now reduced the size of the bags we carry on the plane. It takes more of our daily allotment of energy circuits (fuel) to carry around heavy beliefs and the tighter we have them packed the heavier it is to carry. We could put those energy circuits to better use resulting in slowing down the aging process. If we spend all our energy circuits dragging around our beliefs, it will make us tired, gray and sick.

WHAT IS THE LANGUAGE OF THE SUBCONSCIOUS? WHERE IS THE KEY?

Say Thank You! It's not the spoken word as much as the individual's belief in oneness, with themselves and others. It's not "please" nor "can you." It's definitely not, "I need, I want." It's affirming that our request is already present in our world at this moment in time. In a quantum frequency, we are automatically manifesting the thoughts we are projecting. Now our only job is to align to the frequency we have put in motion and say, "Thank you." We align by believing it's already happened before we physically see the vision in solid form. Whatever thought we project into the Quantum Field is mirrored back to us instantly, good or bad!

The key to the door of the subconscious is a frequency of belief allowing us to access all subconscious programs. Just like our car door remote opens our door and not everyone else's door in the parking lot, our frequency is our vibrational fingerprint and ours alone. How do phone calls stay separate when so many are calling at the same time? That question has always made me scratch my head searching for an answer. I still don't know the answer, but what I do know is that it works pretty well without my knowing the specifics. By the simple action of calling someone on a smartphone we give it credibility; we hold the proof in our hand. There is a built-in assurance because it has become a normal activity in our life, but think about someone a hundred years ago and what his/her response would be to a smartphone.

Once the frequency is activated by our beliefs, (a shift in consciousness) we have access to levels of our existence that were not available before; mainly because we were unaware they existed. With access comes knowledge made available to us through channels in our mind centers that were opened and reconnected by the activation.

Now that we know how the unconscious controls a large part of our everyday activities, we need to understand how we can connect to the Field around us. Our thoughts connect and move through the Field of Light, finding its destination. Once contact has been made the energies will do what they do best, according to the consciousness that created them.

In the Quantum Field our projection already exists because time is not linear; it is past, present and future existing as one. Our job is to realize we can make a quantum leap into what we truly desire and leave our outdated beliefs behind. If we are not willing to change we will keep having the same Groundhog Day experience over and over. Our thoughts will keep producing fertilizer as we scan the horizon, looking to blame someone else for all the unwanted events showing up in our life.

QUANTUM FACTS

The fundamental laws of quantum physics say that an event in the subatomic world exists in all possible states until the act of observing or measuring it "freezes" it or pins it down to a single state. This process is known as the collapse of the wave function, where "wave function" means the state of all possibilities. Although nothing exists in a single state independently of an observer, you can describe what the observer sees, but not the observer. We included the moment of observation in the mathematics, but not the consciousness doing the observing. There was no equation for an observer. If a human observer settled an electron into a set state, to what extent did he or she influence reality on a large scale? The observer effect suggested that reality only emerged from a primordial soup like the Zero

Point Field with the involvement of living consciousness. The logical conclusion was that the physical world existed in its concrete state only while we were involved in it.

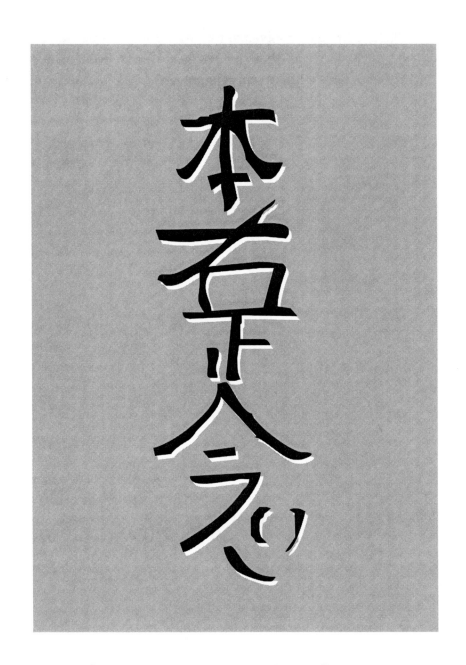

HON SHA ZE SHO NEN

5

Is It Necessary To Use The *HON SHA ZE SHO NEN* Symbol For Distance Healing?

Hon Sha Ze Sho Nen **Absent** Healing Symbol (AHS)

Distance healing can and has been done without using the second degree Reiki symbol, *Hon Sha Ze Sho Nen*. The *Hon Sha Ze Sho Nen* symbol makes it easier to transfer the energy from one place to another. We can cup our hands and get a drink of water or we can use a glass. The glass is the more efficient way to hold water just as the *Hon Sha Ze Sho Nen* is the more efficient way to connect to another person when sending energy. It opens an ether tube of Light from your consciousness to the other's consciousness. I am a Reiki Master and have the *Hon Sha Ze Sho Nen* in my healing toolbox so it gets used every day on me and clients. Sometimes I am watching TV and feel my knees wanting some love and I put them in a tube of Light and love while watching *Jeopardy*.

The *Hon Sha Ze Sho Nen* when spoken or written is a key that opens a doorway of energy that formulates an ether tube of Light connecting us by our spoken command to anyone two feet to 2000 miles or more away. It's also referred to as the absent healing symbol, meaning the person we are working with doesn't have to be in our presence to receive the energy.

Working daily with the energies of Reiki since 1995 has allowed me to increase my vibrational communication to all Usui Reiki Symbols, especially the Absent Healing Symbol (AHS). I would love to share with you the many ways I use this powerful symbol. It's as useful as "a pocket on a shirt."

REIKI SYMBOLS ARE KEYS TO DOORWAYS OF ENERGY

We are dealing with intelligence when keying the Reiki symbols. There is a specific energy frequency associated with each symbol. Each specific energy frequency gives each symbol the properties of being a Key frequency that can access energy in the Universal Light that holds the same vibration. Our front door key will not open our neighbor's front door, just as the vibrational key for the Power Symbol will not initiate the vibrational key for the Absent Healing Symbol (AHS) or Mental Emotional Symbol. Each symbol has its own code vibration that's activated to its optimal level by drawing the symbol and speaking the symbol's name (key) three times. I have found that after we become familiar with the symbols and have built a rapport, we can activate the key energy with our thoughts. There needs to be a congruency present with the symbols for this to be effective. I will say that Reiki Energy will flow continuously without being keyed once we are attuned, but we will not have any specific key energy at work during this type of activation. The intelligence within the key value of the symbol will always be in agreement with us if our intentions are pure and direct.

WHAT EXACTLY DOES THE HON SHA ZE SHO NEN DO?

What is its key job? The purpose of the *Hon sha Ze Sho Nen* is multifaceted. It will connect our Light Intention to the Light Intention of someone thousands of miles away or sitting in the chair in front of us. It holds the integrity of the intent over great distances and allows us to interact with the frequencies of Light required for each connection. My intent is always to allow each vibration necessary for each individual healing.

All the practices I am revealing to you are things I have learned over the years by using the *Hon sha Ze Sho Nen* daily. When you partner with and acknowledge this energy and its equal intelligence, you build a strong bond. I released all known information about the *Hon Sha Ze Sho Nen* and started listening to the vibration of the symbol. It is far more useful when you give it freedom from protocol.

You can place a second AHS (Absent Healing Symbol) over the placement of the first symbol for additional clarity and more energy. When working with back problems, I have placed the AHS on every vertebra of the spine and have allowed the AHS to hold the specific frequency that each vertebra requires. A damaged vertebra requires a frequency different from a healthy vertebra. I usually add additional Light to each AHS tube with the intention of surrounding and cushioning each vertebra, allowing the necessary movement and healing to take place. Try this approach and see what happens during the process. The AHS seems to cushion the damaged area, relieving the pain of our client; and we can command the AHS symbol to stay in place as long as it is required for the healing to take place. Remember we can speak to the intelligence of the symbol. Command means we are giving the energy permission to go to work, not bossing anything around.

It isn't necessary to tell the energy what to do; our job is to key in the symbols and hold the energy in place permitting the known frequency to reset to a perfect healthy balance. The more we can allow by moving out of the way of the energy, the better the outcome of each healing.

Get creative with the *Hon Sha Ze Sho Nen*; it has its own intelligence and will only do what it does best. There have been studies of sending healing energy to participants in the next room and 900 miles away and both received the energy at the same time. Cell phones are the easiest way to explain how the Light of God works. We are not connected to anything tangible when we use a cell phone, but we are able to talk to someone in another country or in another room just the same. The *Hon Sha Ze Sho Nen* works the same way and is far more dependable, never dropping the connection until we are finished.

We can travel back in time to an event in the tube of Light and set in motion the energy of change by forgiving the past. I have seen it work in my life as well as the lives of others as we reap the rewards of forgiveness. The world around us will out-picture the change. Only then can we stop living our history that has kept us locked into the victim consciousness of low vibrational thinking. Be victorious as we allow ourselves to grow from all the fertilizer that has piled up in our life. Recognizing the summer, fall, winter, and spring of our life. It's called change! Change can be a very good thing.

I received a fortune cookie the other day that read, "A man that has never made any mistakes has not lived a worthwhile life." I put it in my pocket and added it to my collection of wise sayings.

We can travel to the future and put an energy field in place that will be beneficial to an upcoming event such as a medical procedure, celebration event, speaking engagement, evaluation, family visit, lawyer appointment, etc. The energy field will not change anything, but will hold our intent in place until the event occurs. A warning here: be careful to send the Highest Light vibration we are capable of holding. If we are worried, that will be the vibration we will be sending.

I send my Light before me everywhere I go and when it is something really important to me I send it in a tube of Light, which will anchor my intent in place and hold the integrity of the intent until the event occurs. Going to the dentist is one of my least favorite things so I always send a tube of Light to everyone present in the office and to every tooth in my head, and give permission for all energies necessary for a perfect outcome to be anchored in place. When I arrive, the pathways have been cleared for all God-Energies to be present and working on my behalf.

ENERGETIC BREAKDOWN FOR *AHS* HON SHA ZE SHO NEN

- *Hon Sha Ze Sho Nen* is related to the bridge between two worlds.
- *Hon Sha Ze Sho Nen* is Chinese. This symbol is the connection for sending a distant healing energy…time and space do not affect this symbol.
- *Hon* - center, essence, origin, intrinsic nature.
- *Sha* - shimmering light.
- *Ze* - advancing, correct course, moving ahead.
- *Sho* - target, integrity, enlightened sage.
- *Nen* - stillness, the deepest part of.

I usually draw the symbol into my palms or visualize the symbol moving from my third eye to my palms. Once my palms are activated, I command the *Hon Sha Ze Sho Nen* by speaking the name three times and giving the command to go to work. Commanding means giving the energy permission to work while activating the intelligence in whatever action is taking place. The Power Symbol is great for energizing your body before a healing by placing the PS into each chakra and sensing the change. You will know the activation is complete when you feel a flow of energy moving through your physical body. Some may only feel a slight tingle while some feel the flow through all seven major chakras and even into the eighth, ninth and tenth chakra above the crown.

For instance, I might layer the Power Symbol on top of the initial symbol I have keyed. When this registers with my conscious mind I then give permission for my subconscious mind to install the programs necessary to receive the most benefit of all symbols and to run them.

Where Do I Begin; Are There Key Steps In The Process?

1. You have to believe that it's possible.
2. Release all fear related to failure.
3. Release your hold on all dogma relating to distance healing.
4. Allow the consciousness of God-Light to flow without your intervention.

Distance healing is not a way to diagnose; it's a way to change a vibration that is off within the body. It is not meant to deter us from seeing a doctor or getting assistance from the medical community. Rather, it assists us in clearing our mind in order to make the best decisions and to release us from the shackles of fear of the unknown.

Forgetting everything we've learned about healing until now is a great way to create a space for new instruction to download. Letting go of old outdated programs encourages the mind to accept new concepts as they are presented. We are bound to a point by the collective unconscious of our family and the world as we remain bound to the beliefs of others until we decide that we have a mind of our own. This comes from realizing those around us never open their minds to the scientific possibilities of what is being presented before them and only accept the reality of what they know. They would never have stepped on board the *Santa Maria* with Christopher Columbus because of the uncertainty involved.

No one understood about microorganisms until we had a microscope to see them. The germ hypothesis was inconceivable to the average person. How can anything I can't see be a threat to me? They had nothing in their knowing that would allow this information any comprehension; it had to be a demon possessing the body causing the illness, not a germ. Most everyone had heard about demon possession and spells being cast against someone causing illness, but few knew about germs. We all have a tendency to go with a known belief instead of stepping out with our own belief; however, there comes a time when we let go of the norm and embrace supernatural living. Only then can we start living our blissful truth.

I was in church every Sunday morning, Sunday evening and Wednesday night and didn't understand supernatural living. You would have thought having that much exposure to church doctrine could possibly lead to enlightenment, but it didn't. I knew my mind and knew what it thought because I was the mind. I knew no God could love someone who had thoughts at times that could be labeled as unkind, sexual or sinful. I knew there was no way for me to achieve the virtuous life that was expressed by the doctrine of my church leaders. All I knew to do was judge my shortcomings and hope God would find a way to overlook them. I was a sinner!

SELF-REALIZATION

I didn't comprehend what supernatural living meant until I came face to face with God in 1995. When the true nature of the supernatural aspect of the Divine was revealed to me through my accepting the fact that God loved me just as I was, I didn't have to change one bit for that love to be given. I was set free from the dogma that had dogged me for many years. That's when I found out that God loved all my imperfections without my correcting them. What a relief! I was lovable just as I was. This comes with self-realization as we claim, "I know who I am and I am free to be me." I am not my mother, my father, my siblings, my teachers; I don't have to be anyone but me, now and forever. Thank you, God!

Realizing I was lovable in God's eyes released a burden from my shoulders that had been balancing there for many years. I could breathe freely for the first time in my life and was overcome with a strong feeling of belonging to something supernatural that connected me directly to God. It's personal, this feeling of belonging and is something each of us must attain for ourselves. I can tell you how it feels to belong, but I can't complete your connection to God. You have to become self-realized on your own, knowing you are worthy to receive the love of God without any conditions being met. Realizing you are worthy is the first big step to self-realization.

LIGHT OF GOD = HEALER = EASY BUTTON

I have taught distance healing too many students over the years and they all achieved success. All it takes to be a successful healer is initiation of the healing; we have to start somewhere. Letting go of the outcome is vital to achieve a desired outcome. It's almost as easy as shifting from one foot to the other as we jump from our present space to the desired quantum space where we truly want to be. Change our thoughts and change our reality; remember, it already exists and is in place waiting for us to align our consciousness. If our consciousness holds the truth that it's possible for a healing to happen over great distances, that's what will happen. The ones receiving the energy will validate our success by telling us they felt the shift in their Light. As the healer we must remember that we are there for the healing to take place. The Light of God is doing the healing.

I love positive results when working in the Light of others during distance healing. If we will allow ourselves to believe that it's possible and that we are working with the Divine Principles of the Universe in the Quantum Field, we will be delighted with our results. It's just science at work using a method that everyone can follow to be a successful healer. Remember we're not there to heal the person; we're there for the healing to take place. Time to push the, "It's so easy, God!" button.

HOW TO INITIATE DISTANCE HEALING

I call in the vibrational frequency of the *Hon Sha Ze Sho Nen* for EVERY healing, whether in person or on the phone. I place whomever in a tube of Light, giving additional protection and assistance to the healing taking place. Whenever speaking to anyone on the phone, whether it's a healing or not, the clarity of conversation is magnified. I can see the Light body on the individual just as though the person were in the room with me. I am truly amazed at how simple the process has become! Again I must add that I have built a rapport with the *Hon Sha Ze Sho Nen* Reiki symbol and have great respect and gratitude for the intelligence of the symbol. If used on the phone, we can connect quickly to the Light Body of the individual we are working with.

We can send healing to someone through the *Hon Sha Ze Sho Nen* without the phone line. It's just as easy; however, we will not get the instant feedback from our connection. Activate the *Hon Sha Ze Sho Nen*, repeating the symbol's name three times and then connect to the seeker needing healing by speaking their frequency code, which is their name. Once we have them in the tube of Light we can ask to see their hologram. Once visible we can work in the patterns and interact with the frequencies as they are made visible to us. Everyone can learn this process by practicing it over and over as they send healing to someone. A belief must be apparent for our mind to allow new neural pathways to formulate within the brain. There has to be a starting point for things to move forward or we will remain stagnant and dissatisfied with our progress. I didn't achieve success the first time I looked at something, but I had someone who believed in me and I believed what she told me was possible. I tell you that it's possible and I believe in you. Now keep looking and tell me what you see.

If you have never had a Reiki attunement and don't have the handy dandy *Hon Sha Ze Sho Nen* symbol to work with, you can still initiate a tube of Light. I learned to look in without the assistance of the *Hon Sha Ze Sho Nen* Reiki symbol. I was attuned to Reiki and had the *Hon Sha Ze Sho Nen* in my healing toolbox, but didn't use it until after I learned the process. I found that everything became clear in a tube of Light. We have to come to a realization there is intelligence in all Light and we can interact with the intelligence; this is vastly important. When we wish to use the Light as a venue to reach someone at a great distance, we just thank the Light for assisting us. We don't have to bargain with Light or program Light; we just give permission for the Light to work with us. The Light of God is always ready and available to be of assistance. Our thought has been received by the Light through our thinking as it vibrates into the electromagnetic field around us and plugs our Light into the appropriate Light. This is all made possible through the mind and heart working as one unit of power. The heart takes the emotional vibration of the thought and turns it into an electromagnetic wave as it leaves the heart center. There is intelligence present to interpret what is required and our Light will be connected by a power/ intelligence greater than the mind of man. I know this is hard for some to fathom, but it's the way the intelligence works.

HEART AND MIND POWER COMBO

The heart does more than regulate the flow of blood through the body. We never think about the heart's being such an active part of our thinking, but the heart's importance needs to be understood. At the same time our thoughts leave the mind, the electromagnetic pulse encoding of the heart enters the electromagnetic field around us. The heart has already interpreted the emotional value of the thought; once the connection is made the thought travels to wherever it's intended through the quantum field. A lot of explaining to the Light about what needs to occur is not necessary, because of the vastness of the Universal Light knowledge available. Whatever is in the consciousness connecting the Light will be sent in the Light. That's why it's important for the healer to realize he or she is not there to heal, but to be present as the healing takes place. The healer's main job is to have a clear mind and clear directive, knowing they have connected to infinite possibilities in the field.

Wouldn't it be nice to send love to someone serving in the military that may be lonely or fearful? We can put Light around them for protection instead of all the fear we might have been sending to them. Sending love to a child while at school in another state will be beneficial to their wellbeing and will assist them in staying on an even flow.

Sending Light ahead of us is a good thing! We can start out by reserving parking spaces to see how it works. I get tickled when I drive into a parking lot that I have sent my Light before me and find the perfect place to park. I get the eye roll from my daughter and her husband because of it sometimes. Once I was to meet them at a theater in Nashville for a movie where there is one parking lot in front of the theater and another lot nearby for a mall. They were out front waiting as I pulled into a parking spot directly in front of the theater entrance. They had parked at the mall because the theater lot was full. I could see the head shakes and the eye rolls as I got out of the car.

Love is a powerful element of Spiritual Technology that can be used without fear of interfering with another's Light. I am talking unconditional love with nothing attached and definitely with no requirements or judgments hidden under well-meaning platitudes. All I do to send love is see the person as Light, smiling as their light gets brighter, all the time realizing I am communing with God. We can do it and they will feel our love no matter how far away we may be from them.

HOW RESPONSIBLE AM I FOR A PERSON'S HEALING?

The healer sets the standard and has certain responsibilities to the seeker. The healer holds the space and keeps it at a level for the healing to take place. Let's take a hot skillet and bacon and eggs into the quantum field for a minute. The healer is the consciousness observing the bacon and eggs frying. The seeker is the bacon and eggs. The consciousness of God is the hot skillet on the burner. God holds the contents in His skillet and the power to make breakfast happen. The healer may turn on the heat under the skillet, but is not the power of the heat; the healer is the observer who turned the knob to allow the power to work. The healer's job is to activate the process and remove the bacon and eggs from the skillet when they are done. Now, how much responsibility does the healer have? Knowing how to turn on a stove, recognizing when the bacon and eggs are ready and not taking credit for being the hot skillet.

My true responsibility as a healer is having the ability to realize the presence of God in every moment of my life. When I attain this objective I have arrived at the place of miracles where God is! This is the home of no separation, only Oneness with the Divine. We must realize that there is no space between us and God. Where does God stop and start in your world? God doesn't stop or start! God is!

Don't push God to Sundays or have God live in some unreachable place. God is all-consuming—all-powerful—everywhere—all-the-time present in your life, right now! God doesn't sleep, cry, judge, whine, or punish. God is! When we suffer it's not God punishing us; it's because we have activated cause and effect somehow. We become so dedicated to a particular form of thought that we can't see the forest for the trees. We have made choices that brought some consequence into our life. We are responsible for our actions. My Granny Hughes always said, "You reap what you sow." Who would have thought Granny knew about Karma?

Now try to wrap your mind around this just a little: we and God are the same. I know, you are thinking, "If God and I are the same, He has some explaining to do about Saturday night." God allows us to do crazy stuff and that is when we experience cause and effect. If we learn from our up-close and personal experience with cause and effect, our Soul will evolve and hold more God Light to assist ourselves and others. It's like looking in the mirror after our bath and taking responsibility for the reflection, knowing that we are the one who supersized the fries and gobbled a baker's dozen glazed doughnuts. We can't keep pointing our finger at "The Burger Palace and Doughnut Shop" when we should point at ourselves. God didn't turn evil and give you a hankering for something fried. It's our responsibility to pick a Red Delicious Apple for a snack and have a nice salad for lunch. It makes God smile when we make good food choices; if you don't believe me, look in the mirror and see God smiling back at you. Maybe we should mesh with this all-consuming—all-powerful—everywhere—all-the-time presence in our life? I don't see how it could hurt to have the realization that God is sleeping on my pillow and brushing my teeth in the morning.

WHERE IS YOUR PARKING LOT?

We are responsible for whatever we put into the Field and it is reflected back to us, immediately. It's not delayed for two weeks, but happens right now. That's why it's important to realize where we have parked our mind at all times. This concerns every thought we have: not just the nice, appropriate thoughts, but also the ones that we would rather others not know about. We like to think that if we don't say it out loud or it's not saved like the Nixon tapes, we can't be held accountable. *Au contraire*! It will catch up to us as we start receiving the frequency we send in the Light. When we continually talk about people in a negative fashion behind their backs, we can count on receiving the same treatment from others. You will probably feel a shudder run through your body when I tell you that everything you think and say about your mother-in-law is known on some level! Every time we say something behind anyone's back, good or bad, they know on some unconscious level. They will feel when you don't like them. The smile on your face combined with obligatory words will not fool them for long.

WHAT PULLS US IN OPPOSITE DIRECTIONS AT TIMES?

We constantly let the ideas about the outer world shape our neural networks, but our inner world (network) need not be dependent on what is happening around us. Whatever's in the collective unconscious doesn't have to rule our world; we can rise above the collective truth, allowing the necessary paradigm shift to happen. When this occurs there is a knowing that whatever is showing up in our world is there for a Divine purpose. How we react to this Divine purpose's showing up in our world is how we will evolve. If we have the mind of Sherlock we will look for clues to see what's up. If not, we will keep creating the same experience over and over.

Have you ever heard the statement, "Suffering exists only because we become attached to a particular form?" What exactly does that mean? I had to do the head-scratch thing as I thought about the definition. After much pondering I finally realized it had something to do with how I viewed my world: how strongly I felt about the thousands of beliefs I had stockpiled over the years, feeling somehow they were all factual and held a strong truth. Well, I have found my assumptions may not have been accurate concerning my beliefs. There has been some serious shuffling of information in my mind centers lately as I delete the old, making room for more supernatural thinking. I don't know about you, but I'm not a fan of suffering.

THE REAL ROAD TO HAPPINESS IS PAVED WITH WRINKLES

What is happiness anyway? Webster's definition: a mental or emotional state of well-being characterized by positive or pleasant emotions ranging from contentment to intense joy.

How do we get to this emotional state of being? Why not find some truly happy people and ask them how they found intense joy and happiness? I'm not talking about superficial happiness, as when someone has just fallen in love or bought a shiny new car. I'm talking about being happy even if you had a fender-bender on the way to work or the washing machine stopped on the spin cycle and gave up the ghost. Or when you have peace, no matter what is happening in your world. My suggestion is, if you want dependable solid information; find someone with heavy laugh lines connected to a few deep wrinkles. They have let go of the need to please everyone and shoot from the hip in most every situation. Wrinkled people are not as invested in pleasing the general public and will tell it like it is. It's not that wrinkled people don't care; it's that they have been there and done that and experienced the consequences. They have initiated cause and effect more times than you have fingers and toes; they know things. Well-seasoned people know not to touch a hot burner. You can't be around that long without learning something worth sharing. Wisdom comes with age through years of experience.

I really didn't understand what real happiness was until I was almost sixty years old. At the time I was heavily invested in fixing everyone around me, molding them to be more like me. Thank God

I wasn't effective with that one! Not sure the world is ready for a town full of clones of me.

Through the grace of God I stumbled upon teachings that helped me understand that everyone is perfect as they move through their life experience. I was supposed to love them where they were, not where I wanted them to be. I learned that fixing others to fit my model was exhausting work and the only model I have the right to change is mine. Seeing everyone as an expression of God saved me in so many different ways, giving me more free time to express my joy and happiness.

BECOMING A CRUSTY OLD CRONE

In 2009 I created a workshop called: "In Search of the Goddess - Embracing the Crone." I was surprised to find out how many people of crone age didn't want to be called a crone. The definition of crone, from the word "crown:" an old woman; archetype: wise woman. Hag used to mean "a holy one" from Green Hagia, as in Hagiolatry, worship of saints. (However, "hag" in the collective unconscious means an old, thin and ugly woman or witch.)

It's time to give power back to the wise old crones and hags. I will stand and be the wise old Crusty Crone, willing to share my truth with the younger generation. There wouldn't be as many wars if you asked a crone if fighting were the right thing. The Iroquois Nation was required to ask the grandmothers of the tribe if they should go to war and if the grandmothers said no, they had to meet in council again and come up with another way of dealing with a situation. Always seek out a wrinkled person for advice; the more wrinkles they have, the wiser the counsel.

CREATING A HEALING SPACE: LOCATION MATTERS

When planning your space to facilitate healings, your location is important to achieve a successful outcome over the years. Find a designated area, someplace only you will utilize, and it will assist in anchoring an energy that will be beneficial. You will find over time that the space you have set aside and appointed for healing will change in vibration. Once the energy is anchored for spiritual endeavors it becomes easier to see and assist others in changing their vibration to a healthy frequency. We must be very respectful of the energies of God that are present and willing to work with us on a daily basis. This area will be beneficial for sending any kind of healing Light to others.

Keep a blank wall or hang a mystical tapestry in your chosen area. I have a lotus and Om symbol tapestry on my wall. I highly suggest you start out with a blank wall for your first viewings, an area about four or five feet square. Remove any pictures that are not conducive to healing and maybe add a few things that resonate with you that carry the higher vibrations of Light. Some people have a Bible, some use crystals, some use cryptic symbols, some use pictures of Saints, Buddha or Ascended Masters. Whatever is spiritual to you, use it in your space, always returning to this same space to tap into the frequencies of God that you have anchored. If we always use the same space when we are communicating with someone through the inner planes or in person, we will soon be able to feel an energetic imprint.

While living in Nashville, I usually did interviews with clients at the kitchen table, so looking at their hologram in the blank space above the stove became a natural process. I also found that being in the kitchen had a calming effect on everyone. We would talk as they sipped a cup of steaming hot mint tea made from the pot of fresh mint growing at the front steps. While we talked they would unconsciously reveal what needed to be addressed during their session. I always returned to the same area while working on spiritual affairs. This guaranteed a successful viewing session with clients. Once you lock the energy in place, it will stay as long as you support what you have built, sort of like maintenance on your home or watering your plants.

When I was growing up we did everything in the kitchen. I feel it was more than being close to snacks; I think it was a common ground where we felt nurtured and safe from the world. Be creative in your thinking as you find a safe space to talk to clients and try not to be bound by traditional thought about what is appropriate.

"Looking In" has evolved over the years to seeing the caller as a hologram and being able to move energy in their field miles away from my location. I can't tell you exactly when I started seeing holograms. I stumbled upon the technique as I viewed the caller by placing their form on the wall, and this process has evolved over time. It's the same as using the click and drag on the computer; you take the Light encodement frequency of the individual and move it to a blank background.

Having done this for many years, it's easy for me to get to that place of viewing whatever I need to see, whether it's viewing someone in the *Han Sha Ze Sho Nen* or looking in while driving to work to see if I left the stove on. Once we plug into Zero Point Energy we're in a God Zone, a place where miracles happen and we can accomplish anything our mind can believe.

Additional neural pathways must be created in the mind in order for us to make sense of a new reality. These pathways are created through our experiences as we interact with others. I feel strongly that we are working on a Soul's level most of the time when learning new things. When we allow ourselves to ponder about what is evolving around us instead of accepting things as they are, some of the filters are removed by the new frequency and clarity is possible.

WEIRD DISTANCE HEALING ACTIVATION

My sister Geraldine will often call to tell me how bad she feels or what level of pain she is experiencing. It's just part of the conversation as we talk about what is going on in our world as sisters. Note that I have not put her in an ether tube of light or initiated a healing for her pain to diminish during our conversations, but her energy changes just by our having a conversation. She will tell me after about thirty minutes that she feels better and that she will talk to me later.

I often thought, "How does that happen by conversing on the phone?" She didn't ask for a healing, she only related to me that she had pain. What I have figured out over the years is that the closer we are to people, the more Light we have established between us that connects us on many levels. This connection facilitates an action connected to the unconscious mind, the part of us that does things that we don't consciously think about. We never think about breathing, blinking or blood flowing because our autonomic nervous system is taking care of this vital aspect of our life. The same thing applies to our never thinking about the activation of programs running in the unconscious that some call supernatural. These same programs work freely, just like the program for breathing happens without our telling the lungs what to do. My conversation with Geraldine activated what she needed by her voice speaking some code that put it into action on another plane of existence.

Don't you find it interesting that all it took was a connection made through the phone call? A program was activated by my interaction on a conscious level putting things in motion on an unconscious level. I find it amazing that we have components within us that are capable of doing such things. Years ago I would have thought you were nuts if you tried to explain this to me. You would have gotten an eye-roll for sure. Now it's my turn to receive the eye rolls as I explain how healing can happen on your smartphone. Do you think if we put the process in an app it would be better received? Probably! I'll work on it!

7

Is There A Distance When The Energy Is No Longer Effective?

The answer is a big fat "NO!"

QUANTUM REALITY OF TIME-SPACE

Since there in no such thing as time in the quantum world and everything exists at the same time, distance has no affect. There have been studies of sending distance healing to people in the next room and to people hundreds of miles away and everyone received the energy at the same time. Distance doesn't matter. I send energy to loved ones in Pakistan all the time. They receive the energy as effectively as my family that lives across town in Tennessee.

When we understand how the quantum field is interconnected we will understand the cohesive action of distance healing. We are connected to everything just by being alive. We are divinely connected to everyone and especially to those we live or work with. When we are sexually involved with a person the connection is enhanced by the coming together of the two energies. These connections form a union that can be wonderfully frightening as we each have the ability to know what the other has in his/her field at all times. This is usually interpreted in the gut feeling category; a feeling that something is "off" in the relationship or something is right in the relationship. We can feel when it's real love and not superficial love, because the information comes from a place where it is defined.

SIGNIFICANT-OTHER CONNECTION

Long before cell phones and beepers, I could pause and think about where my then-husband was and in a little while I would somehow know. It's really not as spooky as it sounds when you apply Spiritual Technology. We had been together as husband and wife for many years and had established many strands of Light that connected the two of us. This connection made it possible to interpret his Light as it traveled through the Field along with my Light. There was no place to hide from my Light as there was no place for my Light to hide from his Light.

When you have a sexual relationship with someone for years, whether married or not, you establish billions of Light connections. When I am clearing lovers who have parted, it looks like limp spaghetti connecting them. Those strings and strands that have created ties through their relationship have to be cut to give freedom for either person to move forward in life. If we don't let go of the ties we will forever find ourselves living in Bill Murray's Groundhog Day. Our past will remain our story until we cut the ties and forgive ourselves and the other person. Taking responsibility for whatever part we may have played in this off-Broadway production will bring us peace. It will literally make us sick and sabotage future relationships if we don't forgive and move all our boxes of junk out of the past.

I have counseled people who separated years before I ever met them and they are just as angry as the day it happened. They were still talking about what he/she did to them ten years before, as they explain how a new lover is now doing the same thing. We will find the same scenario playing out in our world time after time if we don't let go of the past. The experience we have in our relationships resides as an emotional code in our Field and will send out a signal code attracting its twin. This is not a conscious thing; it's the unconscious running our programs. We have to come to a place where we are ready to accept the fact that the mind that created this insanity can create something different; then and only then can things change in our world. First there must be the understanding that this has happened before and we had something to do with the creation. Your Soul wants you to realize what is going on so you will learn whatever lesson is appearing in real time.

MORPHOGENESIS OF DISTANCE HEALING

Rupert Sheldrake's book <u>Morphic Resonance</u> explores morphogenesis and how it works. I saw it in action during the 2010 Deepwater Horizon spill in the Gulf of Mexico. That environmental disaster raised many concerns for our planet and the potential harm that could take place if it wasn't contained soon. Many groups in the Nashville area were meditating, sending Light at the same time. I sent out a call for all who had the time, to gather at a park for a group meditation. As we stood together with our hands linked in oneness we sent our love to the Gulf of Mexico, for the best outcome. Having the gift of sight, I could see the meditative thought leave our group of about thirty people and take the form of an ethereal smoke ring as it traveled into the spheres. I then noticed a huge formation like a gigantic smoke ring that our little ring of love and light attached to. It became part of the greater whole as it meshed into oneness with the existing Light. I realized that we had become part of a morphic field established by all the prayers being sent from all over the world for the best outcome in this situation. Seeing it mesh together was so unique and helped me understand the intelligence of morphogenesis at work and how Spiritual Technology is a viable tool for change.

This one experience helped validate to a greater degree how valuable distance healing is to the ecosystem of planet Earth. Distance didn't matter as we sent our love to the Gulf of Mexico. I know it was beneficial and assisted the environment on land and in the water. Send Love to the Amazon rainforest thanking God for its preservation.

Gratitude is one of the highest forms of Love. Being in gratitude while sitting and realizing God is with us every moment of the day changes the frequency of the Universe. We don't need to pray for something to happen; we need to thank God for whatever is happening, knowing somehow that God is in charge. Being in gratitude is prayer in itself. Gratitude is that one-size-fits-all kind of miracle; use it extravagantly!

STRING THEORY AND DISTANCE HEALING

Don't you think the ability to heal over great distances involves String Theory? Think about the connections that need to be made to send healing Light to the other side of the world. It's easier to accept distance healing in our hometown or up the road a couple of hundred miles or so. Connecting to the Light of someone over 6,000 miles away is harder to grasp. There is nothing in our gray matter that will allow us to sort this out intellectually. That's when we have to have faith: when we have to believe it's possible without knowing *how* it's possible.

In my opinion, I feel that we can send healing energy to a Martian.

Kevin in Peru

Kevin lives in Peru part of the year while his good friend Jeff lives in Nashville. They send healing energy every day to one another. Distance doesn't matter when you combine your strings and strands to the strings and strands of Universal Light. Stir in a little unconditional Love with the intent of blessing someone and you have just baked a delicious outcome for healing.

Jeff in Nashville

Kevin feels the good vibes being sent from Nashville over 3000 miles to Peru. He knows for a fact that distance doesn't matter. Knowing you are connected regardless of how far away you may be from the ones you love keeps the heart strong and a big smile on your face. Jeff feels the Light of God coming from Kevin to Nashville. He is a believer in Quantum Entanglement: two particles behaving as one no matter how far apart they may be. (Spooky action at a distance as Einstein called it.) Jeff is in agreement with being tangled in the quantum field with Kevin's Light 3000 miles away.

SENDING DISTANCE HEALING TO THE FUTURE

Distance Healing 1,145 miles away. I catered parties for twenty years and every time we had an outdoor wedding or any social event it was always inconveniently problematic. Not just once or twice, but always! It was the weather, the terrain or the host, and God forbid you got the Grand Slam Triple!

Knowing this about my catering days will assist you in understanding the following account of distance healing. A friend came for a session to assist with correcting the energies present in her life. During our conversation I cringed when she told me her daughter was getting married and it was an outdoor wedding in September. With emotions and hundreds of things that have to come together at once to have a perfect outcome, it's almost impossible to have a wedding without a few mishaps. I knew I could send Light to an event in the future and offered to assist her in sending Light to the future wedding. She was all for giving it a try; we decided it couldn't hurt. (This also works well for a visit to the dentist, lawyer's office, etc.)

I gave her instructions on how to send her intentions through an either tube of Light, telling her she was responsible for activating the program every day or two before the event. She left and as she promised, she sent Light every day to the future event.

Outcome: everything was ideal for the wedding. The weather was clear and perfect and the ceremony was flawless, without a glitch. The bride was happy with her perfect day and no one got drunk and fell into the cake. The bride's mom is now a believer and very pleased with the outcome. She sends her Light before her regardless of what the event may be.

RESPONSIBILITY FOR THE LIGHT I SEND

When I send my Light before me in a distance healing format it clears everything that may be considered low vibrational frequencies. This happens on a daily basis, not once or twice a year. My intent becomes the Light projected through my thoughts and finds its connection in the Field around me. Once the connection is made it takes on a life of its own. This is wonderful! However, I am bound by the laws of the Universe and held accountable for my thoughts. If I slip down into a low vibrational frequency by thinking that I know what is best for someone else, my ego is in charge, not my Higher Self. If I am judging their actions or what they are wearing, I am responsible for everything that shows up in my life; that was arranged by my thoughts. Whenever we know what is best for someone else we are not coming from a place of love; we are coming from a place of self-righteous opinions. We should never have opinions. We should have only love.

While putting together the final stages of a workshop I will receive validation that I am sending information into the Light. Days before the workshop is to be announced I start receiving calls about whatever I am about to offer in public. I have started calling it, "Advertising in God Light," because I hadn't told anyone verbally about what I was about to offer and they have already started responding. Somehow they received the information through their connection to me in the Universal Light. There are so many levels of consciousness at work at all times and we don't have a clue as to how it works. All I know is it works and does its thing and we benefit from this unknown source when we send the correct Light into our sea of quantum fields.

This also works with the Light of people you have never met, when their Light is searching for whatever vibration you have put into the Field. As their thoughts go into the Field they will find your vibrational message and connect with whatever you have going on. I added two new workshop attendees recently as I was planning for a workshop. They are not sure how they found my website, but I am. String Theory is alive and well in my world as it connects on the unseen level.

Whatever I am projecting into the Light makes itself known from the simple to the incredible, every day. If I need help moving a piece of furniture, all I do is think about the piece being moved and someone shows up to move it for me. Whenever my income slows down I sit and talk to the Light. After a few minutes of conversation I thank the Light for listening and expect a change to occur in the flow of money in my world and it does. Yes, it's that simple to correct our Light to a higher frequency. Once we realize we have plugged into a lower vibration, for whatever reason, we can make a change. Acknowledging the situation is a way of correcting the Light. This is simplified after we learn to take responsibility for what we are experiencing at all times. Whatever is showing up in our world is our creation and we must own it by recognizing we have programs running that need to be cancelled. When we choose not to hide behind the illusion of, "I had nothing to do with this" and take ownership for whatever is happening, we can make a change.

Distance truly doesn't matter as the strings and strands of Light connect us to infinity and beyond. I know it works as it out-pictures in my world daily in simple and incredible ways. I know what it feels like to be blessed.

8

Is It Necessary To Send Distance Healing More Than Once To The Same Person?

THE ANSWER IS "YES"

It could take more than one distance healing if the person delays a request for help and if he/she is really sick. The influence of the people around him/her sometimes determines how fast he/she will heal.

There are programs of beliefs within our unconscious running 24/7 that operate on their own without consulting the conscious mind. We have created these programs over the years when we made certain truths. The subconscious stored them all and will keep running them daily until we have a shift in our conscious mind telling us that it's just an illusion and to let it go. We were making truths according to what was happening to us by the time we are six years old. Scary stuff huh? After we reach six years old the brain matures and so does our view of the world. We made truths at six that we still react to even if we are fifty-six. That's definitely scary! Think about the fears you had at six or seven; when mom left you for a week to take care of her sick mother, you felt abandoned and created a program with your new truth. In your young mind it was very true: my mom doesn't love me. Your adult mind understands and can rationalize what's going on, but not a six-or seven-year-old mind. Now you have a program of abandonment anchored as a truth within your subconscious. Every time something with the same vibration happens we add it to the truth we made at six. These truths keep piling up over the years, every time we react when the program is activated. See how easy it is for us to make programs? It's our adult job to recognize that a program is running and address whatever emotional vibration that is showing up in our world. It's very simple to change the program when you allow yourself to take responsibility for whatever is showing up today. Once we claim our part, we can initiate a new, more beneficial program that will bring stability to our emotional body. Yippee!

GOD LIGHT IS REAL

Can there be intelligence greater than our own mind; an intelligence that will change the cells within our body? On some cold lonely evening go to your bookshelf and open Dr. Bruce Lipton's book, "The Biology of Belief" and expand your awareness about what you are truly made of and how your community of cells can change from unhealthy to healthy by changing your beliefs. It may help you understand why you are ailing from an illness that has arrived in your life, unintentionally invited. He took cloned stem cells and realized there was intelligence within each cell as his scientific mind found the spiritual investment within our bodies. He realized that the environment of the cell was the key to our health. When unhealthy cells left alone in a petri dish healed, he knew a higher intelligence within each of the cells was the only explanation. His studies prove there is intelligence available to all and we have the ability to plug into that intelligence. When we remove the separation created by our programs of beliefs between the conscious mind and superconscious mind, we have the ability to tap into the mind of God: Zero Point Energy.

A shift in the Light frequency has to take place for someone to experience a healing. All I do is correct the frequency that is off. I am not there to heal; I am there for the healing to take place. All I am doing is realizing God. God is real.

The healer carries a huge responsibility for having the correct vibrational belief so that a healing can take place. The one being healed can assist by believing in the healer's ability to connect to the highest vibrational healing Light, making it possible for his/her healing, just like in Lipton's petri dishes when the cells healed on their own.

As humans, we unplug from our high vibrational God Light and plug into a lower vibration. A lot of times all it takes to correct a vibration is understand that something has happened to your Light and be willing to take responsibility. It's like stepping on the lamp cord and unplugging it from the wall. To correct this malfunction we bend over and plug the cord back into the source of electricity. Changing your Light frequency is almost as simple. Just as you noticed that the lamp gave no light, when you see your Light is not functioning you have the ability to plug back into Source Light. I start having an uneasy feeling when my Light has been compromised. Once I sense that something is off I assist my light in reconnecting to a higher vibrational God Light which brings me back into balance.

Something to note: Light finds its equal and if we are willing to change our Light, our Light will connect to a Superior Light. If we're not willing to change, our Light will find its equal no matter how low the vibration. When we refuse to take responsibility for our Light we may find our Light plugging into frequencies that bring a truckload of crazy our way. We can prevent this from happening when we allow our body to be a meter for changes in the Field around us. If we expect the body to alert us, it will with a gut feeling, a creepy feeling, pressure around the body, smells, etc. It's our responsibility to notice the Light frequency has changed and then do something about the change.

CHANGING THE FREQUENCY OF LITTLE CHILDREN

I have found children easily shift their vibration so they can heal. The younger they are the easier it is to change the frequency that is skewed. When my grandsons were small all I had to do was hold them and they would self-correct. Their little bodies would adjust as I held them on my shoulder rocking them to sleep, with one hand at the base of their neck and the other at the tip of their spine. All I was doing was creating a circuit with their spine and sending love to the little sweeties. This technique should be in every mother and grandmother's handbook. It really works by keeping the kids healthy which can mean fewer trips to the doctor. The boys never had tubes in their ears and very few doctor visits.

Now that they are older it takes a little more effort to keep them in balance. They have started making programs and at some point will need to delete some of those running programs. I put them in a tube of God Light even when I am in the same room with them doing a healing, because it assists in keeping the frequencies pure. It takes about five hours to relieve their cold and flu-like symptoms. They will start out listless on the sofa and before you know it they are hungry and wanting to go outside and play. I just love kids!

Repeat: All I do is correct the frequency that is off; I am not there to heal; I am there for the healing to take place. All I am doing is realizing God. God is real!

Lately I have been thinking about what happened to our ability to be happy. Studies have found that when we are young we laugh

300 or more times a day. When we grow into our adult mind we only laugh twenty times a day at most. What happened to the laughter? It gets pushed back and covered with piles of beliefs about what has happened in the past and what is happening in our own world today. If we could look at the situation from the inside out it would resemble one of those programs about hoarders who keep plastic twist ties, old clothes, broken toys and useless junk. We pile so many illusion-based programs on top of our happy programs that the conscious mind can no longer find anything resembling happiness. We may stop to think every now and again about something happy that happened in the past, but it's hard to remove all the layers of beliefs so we can get to the good stuff. However, once we start removing the junk and garbage of the past that no longer serves any purpose in our life we will find all the treasures that were misplaced.

Are you getting a better picture of why it may take more than one session to get the vibrational frequency of some individuals to a level where healing can take place?

WE ARE RULED BY OUR SUBCONSCIOUS PROGRAMS

Just like an iceberg we have a lot under the surface that is not recognized. We have thousands of programs anchored in the subconscious that can be activated by someone's glance, words or actions toward us. We have programs running that can be activated by calling or visiting our home at Christmas or any other time of the year. We may activate a program while driving by the elementary school we attended. We can activate programs when our boss walks by our desk without acknowledging us, or when our best friend buys someone a hamburger and doesn't offer to get us one. Recently I had a call from someone I know who was upset because a friend went to the drive-thru and got burgers for someone and didn't get her one. She activated a program of not being treated fairly: "I must not be worthy of a lousy one-dollar burger."

Why did she react so strongly to her friend's actions? It wasn't because she had been craving the taste of a value meal burger. It was because it activated programs of low self-worth that she had not dealt with. When these programs are activated and we allow ourselves to realize that it's just a program running, it can be changed. Everything that shows up in our daily lives that disturbs the equilibrium of our world is a program running. We are always part of the creation resonating around us. Some of the "truths" we made years ago still hold power over us and will continue to interfere with our day until we finally recognize it's just a program running. When we made these programs by initiating a "truth," it was usually an illusion; it was just "our truth," not the real truth. When we were five or six years old and Mom had to go to work to pay bills, we only knew Mom had deserted us and we felt the separation. We made a program that we can't trust people to always be there to take care of us. Dad may have started driving us to kindergarten or first grade instead of Mom. Now in reality, mom was home every night and cooking dinner, but in our mind she had deserted us, so you made it a "truth." Later the program might activate when we're in a relationship with someone and he/she changes jobs, moves or forgets to tell you they already had vacation plans before you met. This person may buy a car and never ask our opinion and on and on it goes.

Our conscious mind is like the tip of the iceburg that we communicate with in our daily lives. However we are influenced by everything that is under the surface of our conscious mind. Observe how much of the iceburg is under the surface of the water. Only the tip of the iceberg is visible. The same thing applies to our consciousness. There is more under the surface of our consciousness that is affecting our world than we realize. We are being influenced on a daily basis by things beneath the surface. Our evolutionary job is to recognize when there is a program running that the subconscious opened according to the frequency that has been activated by our emotional response to whatever situation is appearing in real time.

We all have running programs of beliefs and these "truths" will surface many times a day making us responsible for what is showing up in our world. Once we recognize it's our virus running amuck, we can delete it and install a new, beneficial program. It stands to reason that if we can create programs by false truths, we can also create different programs with new truths that are beneficial.

HOW TO ACCESS THE SUBCONSCIOUS USING KINESIOLOGY

Kinesiology (muscle testing) is an interesting work used by chiropractors and anyone else wanting to access the subconscious. It's hard to have a conversation with the subconscious, because of the apparent unconscious level of consciousness at work. Do you ever think about blinking, blood flowing, or breathing? If you're like me, you don't; you just take it for granted as something that's supposed to be happening. The subconscious is taking care of business for us, so what's the big deal? There is much going on in the subconscious that most of us are not aware of. What about the programs I have been telling you about? Did we tell the subconscious to store them for us? We say "No," but we should say, "Yes." We give permission for such an action to take place when we make something our truth. The subconscious stores happy memories as programs, as well as programs that are illusion-based. However, we are not haunted or disturbed by our happy programs. In fact, we hardly ever visit these programs and choose to dwell on the negative aspects we have stored.

FINDING DR. CARLSON; A LIFE-CHANGING EVENT

Dr. Carlson is a retired dentist who took a spiritual journey into the field of healing. My first encounter with Kinesiology and Ed Carlson made me realize where my focus was most of the time. The first night of a workshop on forgiveness, he asked all of us to find a perfect moment when everything was wonderful in our lives. "A memory of something so special that it made our heart sing." I couldn't think of a thing! I tried for over ten minutes to come up with something perfect, but events from my youth kept overshadowing any perfect memory. If he had asked me to come up with one hundred not-so-perfect moments, no problem! That's when I realized I wasn't as happy as the smile I showed to others all the time. Wow, my outward happiness was a lie! What an awakening! After sleeping on the question overnight I allowed my conscious mind to remember some good times. Can you believe that it took me all night to allow myself to remember happy times? Can you recall at a moment's notice happy experiences in your life? If you can, you are an exception to the rule. Good for you!

NOTE ABOUT PERFECT MOMENTS

When we are in a perfect moment nothing other than the Light of God can touch us. We are "One" with our Higher Consciousness, the God connected part of ourselves. We can't be sad or depressed in a perfect moment, because of our connection to our Divine Self. It may behoove us to find lots of perfect moments and string them all together like a macaroni necklace and have them ready when life happens. It's a good thing!

I first met Ed Carlson when he was formulating a new series of workshops called Heart Forgiveness. My sister Margaret gifted me with the workshop and I felt like I needed to go. I had a horrible upper respiratory infection that weekend and tried to get out of the experience, but a voice within kept telling me I needed to attend. I went and it was the most enlightening thing I had done in years. I was changed forever!

Dr. Carlson had the privilege of working with Dr. John Diamond, a doctor of Chiropractic Medicine who understood the value of Kinesiology. I was very impressed by my weekend with Dr. Carlson and ten other participants in one of the first Heart Forgiveness Workshops. After my transformation that weekend I knew I had to learn more about Heart Forgiveness and Kinesiology (muscle testing). It took a while for the new information to find a comfortable space in my brain center, but before too long we were BFFs.

You can use the body as a tool, because the body doesn't lie, it will tell the truth every time by going weak when giving a negative response. Dr. John Diamond has a little book called, *"The Body Doesn't Lie"* that I found quite interesting and you may as well. I read that instructors in juvenile detention centers use Kinesiology sometimes to see if kids are telling the truth or not.

THE BASICS OF MUSCLE TESTING

KINESIOLOGY (MUSCLE TESTING)

Merriam-Webster defines kinesiology as the study of the principles of mechanics and anatomy in relation to human movement and their roles in promoting health and reducing disease. Kinesiology has applications for fitness and health, including exercise and rehabilitation, preservation of the independence of older people, disease prevention, disease due to trauma and neglect, and rehabilitating people after disease or injury. Kinesiologists also develop more accessible furniture and environments for people with limited movement and find ways to enhance individual and team efficiency. Kinesiology research encompasses the biochemistry of muscle contraction and tissue fluids, bone mineralization, responses to exercise, how physical skills are developed, work efficiency, and the anthropology of play. *(Concise Encyclopedia)*

SUGAR IS MY FRIEND

Here are a few examples of Kinesiology (muscle testing): There are many triggers that make us go weak in society: if we look at the sign of infinity we will stay strong when muscle tested, but if we look at the two circles separated we will go weak. If someone stands behind us, where we can't see them and frowns while we are being tested, we will go weak. If the same person smiles while we are being tested we will stay strong. Spooky isn't it? That one is really fun and more like a parlor trick. It also holds the truth of how we are affected by the actions of others towards us, while not being aware of their actions. This next example is the personification of mixed messages: if we hold a pack of sugar in a sealed envelope, not knowing what's in the envelope, we will go weak because of all the programming in the collective unconscious of how bad sugar is for us. There is also the side of sugar that is necessary, like the glucose drip in the hospital, and glycogen in the brain (sugar). If you love me you will give me a cake on my birthday and let's not forget chocolate on Valentine's Day. No wonder we go weak with sugar; we are told it is bad for us and will rot our teeth, but if I want to live, if I want my brain to function correctly, I need sugar and if I want to feel loved I expect the gift of sugar. We live in a funny world, don't we? If we think of the many times we see the sugar trigger, we will understand why shopping drains us and cravings start. If we are trying to diet, what do we notice on TV? When we pick up a magazine, what sugar triggers do we see? It's all around us. The key is understanding that we have the ability to make a conscious decision that sugar is our friend, not our enemy. It's just a simple statement that we make to the subconscious and override everything we have learned from society's viewpoint. Now we can go have a brownie without giving our power away. Yippee!

DISCLAIMER

Making sugar your friend doesn't mean that you can have a steady diet of candy bars and cupcakes. Don't tell me I am responsible for the larger-size jeans you had to buy. I only told you to make sugar your friend, not your obsession! Everything in moderation as you yippee down life's pathway!

SIMPLE EXPLANATION OF THE SUBCONSCIOUS

Think of the subconscious as the ground. We can plant belladonna (a poisonous plant) or corn; the subconscious will grow both the poisonous and the edible. It doesn't make judgments about what we are planting and will treat each thing equally. It will never say, "Are you sure you want to plant this poisonous thought here?" It will follow the instruction of the conscious mind. Many of the truths we plant in the subconscious are pure illusion.

When we make judgments through our emotional perceptions they are usually figments of our imagination. We are using the emotional imprints of the truths we have stored in all the programs that activate daily. The subconscious is a busy organization that knows every thought we have stored and it responds instantly to any emotional trigger brought on by whatever we are experiencing in the moment. It does seem at times as if a secret government has control of us, not always in a beneficial manner.

COALESCED TRUTHS

Now is the time to tell you about all the truths we have made that attract their twin frequency. A twin frequency is any emotional response to the established truth that layers a validation of top of the original. Now we have started coalescing one truth on top of another. This happens every time we experience a situation and a program of our truth opens. It doesn't have to be the actual truth, just our truth as it takes up residence in our subconscious.

PONDER THIS

How heavy is one sheet of copy paper? We can lift it with no difficulty, right? How hard is it to pick up a ream of copy paper? Still no problem, especially if you use both hands. But what happens if someone asks us to pick up a case of copy paper and put it in the storeroom? Is it heavy? The truths we make start out like a single piece of copy paper: easy to deal with and not very heavy on the Heart/Soul storage unit. Years of adding layer after layer of the same frequency of truth on top of the original truth will stockpile millions of layers. That's when the weight of all our truths starts to become a burden on the body as we age.

When we keep repeating the same action year after year, holding onto the past with a death grip, the results of this behavior makes itself know through our physical health. We are using more units of energy a day than our body can produce by keeping all these truths alive and well-fed. Where is the extra energy coming from to make this happen? A clue comes from looking in the mirror as we see ourselves age. We keep stealing energy from our vital organs as it takes its toll from the heart, lungs, kidneys, intestines, etc. Now we start to have health issues by keeping all our truths (illusions) alive. Let's have an Irish wake for all our unnecessary truths that are sucking the very life out of us and send them off in a fiery funeral pyre!

SIX-YEAR-OLDS: MYSTERY SOLVED

During muscle testing sessions I noticed that the age of six came up too frequently to be a coincidence. A lot of truths are being formulated at that age. Initially I thought it may be about going to school, because school not only traumatized me, it made me nauseous. Then I thought no, because six-year-olds have already been going to school for a year in kindergarten. The *eureka* moment happened when a group of psychologists started coming for sessions. I found that our brain matures around age six and we start processing information differently. We have a broader view of the world in general. We start seeing Mom with two heads; God and the devil. That's when we start having the comprehension of separation. Until that point we were one with God and the Universe. Don't you find that interesting? I did! I felt like I had won the lottery!

If you ask a five-year-old if he/she is Superman as the child jumps off the back of a sofa, he/she will look at you with wonder and answer yes. We can be anyone at five and believe it, because we are still steeped in Oneness. At six we may still play Superman as our bath towel flaps in the breeze, but we know we are really Andy, Luke or Jim. While demonstrating muscle testing Dr. Carlson asked us to go back to a time when we were five or younger and we all tested positively that we were whatever superhero or character we wanted to be. Don't you think that it's very interesting to be able to go back in time and access the childlike mind? It blew me away the first time I was a part of the demonstration. At five I was strong in believing that I was Cinderella. At six I went weak and no longer believed in Cinderella or Santa. I was marching forward in time, becoming a stable adult, dismissing the fantasies of life.

With all the testing I found that there is also a big hormonal shift in our bodies at age twelve. That's when boys get a deeper voice and girls start developing a more feminine physique. It takes some serious change for that to happen in the body. At twelve we make more sophisticated truths about how we view the world as we start to think about our survival and future. We worry a lot about being accepted by our peers. We run the full gamut of emotions, from happiness to depression in the same day. We are heavily aware of right and wrong at this age. There is also something that seems to change in most of us around seventeen and eighteen. Whether hormonal or environmental, it's a serious change that makes most of us want to go out on our own and leave the nest. We have become so hard-headed by this time that Mom and Dad are not as concerned with keeping us under their wing. They are more than glad to make sure little Suzy and Buster have a college education in a neighboring state to experience dorm life.

VERY PECULIAR: MOM AND GOD ARE THE SAME THING!

I taught a healing class at a bookstore for years, always trying to keep things interesting. One Sunday I thought it would be stimulating to use kinesiology and muscle-test everyone for anger with God. We have all been angry with God at some time in our lives, so it was a good topic. I know, I denied it too, but I was wrong, I went weak when tested. (When you lie, your muscles will weaken with a negative response). There were about twelve of us that day, and we all laughed when the results from eleven of the twelve people revealed that our mothers were the focus of our anger with God. If you think about it, it makes sense; she is our Divine Creator, she gave us birth and we put Mom in a godlike position; when anything goes wrong it has to be her fault. I have muscle-tested adults that received abuse from their fathers and guess who they were angry with? Their mothers! She didn't protect them from the big bad wolf so she received the anger. They also tested strong for angers with God if they were angry with mom. Don't you think that is the most bizarre thing you have ever heard? Well, I do!

The programs we create concerning Mom are the most intriguing. We are bound by the strings and strands of Mom forever. It's crazy stuff! We covered it a little in the family entities section that you may want to read again. I found it fascinating as each session unfolded and revealed the angers toward Mom.

> The mind is complex and dimensional, always working with areas we don't comprehend with our conscious thinking. Take up the slogan; "Boldly go where no mind has gone before."

ANGERS AT MOM RESEARCH

Over the course of six years I amassed a large file of information from people letting go of unconscious programs. The Mom/God thing was the most interesting. Who knew she had two heads? Sounds like a Vincent Price sequel doesn't it, "The Mom with Two Heads?" I can almost hear the eerie music playing in the background and I have a strong desire to look behind me as I type.

Everyone included in this data was over twenty-five years old when the muscle testing was done, and most participants were over thirty-five. I have included the age they were tested, their symptom that was showing up at time of their visit, the age when they made their truth and what that truth was for them at the time. Once a truth has been made, it becomes a program to be activated again and again over the years until we arrive at the conclusion that it's only a program running. When this becomes apparent to our conscious awareness, then and only then can we do something about the program. We then have a choice, to delete the program running or continue our experience. I have selected from the data accumulated over a six-year period about programs running in the subconscious dealing with Mom. If any of the data about mom sounds familiar, maybe it will help you realize you are not alone. Maybe you can cut the old girl some slack and let go of a smidgen of hostility. You may even be a mom now and the same scenario has made its debut in your world as a mom.

This research reveals the truth that was made from their perspective, not necessarily the real truth. They are examples of how we make programs and store them in our Soul computer. The programs will stay active until we recognize them as programs and release them. It shows how we make a truth and how that truth will surface later in life causing the need for a correction in our Light. If we don't recognize that whatever is showing up is only a program that needs clearing, we will have the same experience over and over. It can lead to dysfunction in spiritual, physical and mental areas of our life. It can surface as illness in the physical body.

After a symptom appeared in the body we checked how many anchor points that were invested in each truth. Anchor points are the many times our thoughts layer another truth on top of an existing truth. Most people had made over twenty five thousand anchor points with their belief. If the belief had led to cancer or heart trouble appearing the anchor points would be in the hundred thousand ranges. Now can you see how illness makes an appearance in our world if we don't forgive?

We muscle tested to find the age they made the truth and who was connected to the truth. This research was all about mom so she is the "who" in every truth. After finding the truth and forgiving mom their symptoms disappeared almost every time. Programs need to be cleared as they surface as a symptom. In time people get to the place where they can recognize a program and clear it themselves. That's where we want to be.

Every example listed below is related to angers at Mom. You will see in the research given that some have more than one issue of anger with mom; resulting as dysfunction in the body later in life. Notice the angers at Mom showing up as stomach problems, diabetes, cancer, arthritis, emotional problems etc. Also notice how long after the truth was made before the symptoms of the truth appeared. It has to surface eventually for the Soul to evolve, giving us the opportunity to forgive and let go of the past. Have you ever asked yourself the question; when do we experience enough anger to satisfy us? The answer is never! Waiting on anger to satisfy us is like waiting for a train to take us to the moon. We have to forgive the truth we made and the people involved in that truth to be set free. You can't reason with anger, for it will create more of itself and spread like a cancer.

———•——•———

Female, age 35.

First symptom: stomach problems. At age seven, when her mom was driving the car, the door opened and she was dragged along. This tore the skin off her knees. Her truth: she was not worthy of protection and she didn't feel safe with her mom after the incident. She was very angry with mom.

Second symptom: trust issues. Made a truth at age 12 when she got her period and a neighbor, rather than her mom, had to explain to her what was going on because her mom wasn't there when it happened. Her truth: I'm angry at you mom because you're never available when I need you most; I am alone at difficult times and have to take care of myself.

Third symptom: breast cancer. At age 17, when her stepfather was peeking at her while she bathed. Her mother didn't do anything about it or protect her. Her truth: to be a woman is to be weak and people take advantage of you. "Mom, you could have stopped him."

Fourth symptom: general health problems. Made another truth at 17; anger at her mom who told her she was a "dirty girl" if she wore anything that revealed her figure. Her truth: I can never be a good girl if I wear the clothes I like, so I am doomed to be a sinner.

———•———•———

Female, age 39.

Symptom: problems with tremors in her body. At age twelve, she realized she was invisible in the family as the middle child. Because she was never noticed, she felt left out and alone and had a lot of anger towards her mother. Her truth: angry at her mom because no matter how good I am, I am still invisible to Mom.

———•———•———

Female, age 42.

First symptom: Losing focus in her life. At age 12, she realized her mom could not focus on helping her with the simplest task. She felt her mother never thought about her unless she was standing in front of her. Her truth: out of sight, out of mind. You never think of me; your focus is somewhere else instead of on your daughter.

Second symptom: part of stomach went numb. Mom had double standards for her and her brother and didn't protect her from her siblings. Her truth, made at age 13: very angry at mom because life at home is impossible and hard to stomach.

Third symptom: diabetes. Made a truth at age 13 out of anger with Mom, feeling no sweetness in life. She was afraid to show who she truly was. Her truth: if they know who I am and what my thoughts are, I will never be loved. I will hide behind my mask so I can be loved.

———◆———◆———

Female, age 40.

First symptom: painfully swollen hands. Made a truth at age 12 when her mom told her, "You catch everything that goes around." Her truth: angry because mom acted like she didn't care if she was sick. She just complained that I catch everything that goes around and will always be sick and need to be taken care of.

Second symptom: being invisible in life. Made a truth at age six when Mom paid attention to a sick sibling and left her alone. Her truth: angry at mom because the only attention she got was negative. If they pay attention to my sibling, they will leave me alone. It's safer to be alone and invisible. If they don't see me I won't get into trouble.

Third symptom: anger at Mom. When at age 12 her father beat her and her mother wouldn't stop him. She would think, "Mom, why aren't you protecting me?" Her truth: Mom is weak and I am alone. I can't trust her to take care of me.

Fourth symptom: hypothyroidism. Made a truth at age 17 when she was angry at Mom for giving up on life. She felt hopeless and was told to be quiet and passive around her dad. Her truth: I can't say what needs to be said; I have to hold my tongue.

Fifth symptom: lower back pain. At 16, she saw that Mom was not in charge of their lives. She was supposed to be in charge, but she wasn't. Dad would use the household money and never tell Mom, causing checks to bounce. Her truth: When you get married, you are trapped and don't get any support from the person that should be supporting you. You are on your own even when married.

———◆———◆———

Female, age 31.

Symptom: feeling exhausted/drained. Made a truth at age twelve when she had to do all the work at home for her working mom. She didn't get to be a child. Her truth was: I'm not the mom "it's a thankless job with no benefits and it's unfair. I'm very angry at mom. When do I get to play and be a kid?"

————•———•————

Female, age 37.

Symptom: unable to write music. Made a truth at age six that her mom would not take her seriously. She never recognized her daughter's talent. Her truth: made me angry when they wouldn't believe my dream and could never see me as a performer or songwriter.

————•———•————

Female, age 44.

First symptom: betrayal. At age seven, she felt betrayed by her mom, who said one thing and did another. Her truth: she says she has my best interest at heart, she makes me angry and I can't trust her to take care of me.

Second symptom: fear of the unknown. Made a truth at age eight when kids at school made fun of her because her hair was not properly combed. She was angry at Mom for not combing her hair. Her truth was: I have to figure everything out on my own. I have no guidance, no support, I'm alone and unloved.

Third symptom: blamed for other people's actions at work. Made a truth when at age 12, her mother made her have an abortion after she was raped by a friend of the family. She felt her mom blamed her for the rape. Her truth: I get blamed for other people's actions and things that are out of my control. I am very angry that mom did not protect me.

Fourth symptom: letting go of bad relationships: Made a truth at age 12 when she understood that her mom was present but not there for her; I am on my own in life.

Fifth symptom: unappreciated on the job. While working at McDonald's at age 17, she gave her mother her paychecks, but her mother didn't appreciate the sacrifices she made. Her truth: It makes me angry to never be appreciated for all I do. Can't you see me standing here? Can't you feel my pain?

———•———•———

Male, age 36.

Symptom: lost sight of who I am. When he was six, his mom left to care for her own sick mother and didn't take him with her. His truth: Mother doesn't love me enough to take me with her; she has deserted me and I am upset and alone.

———•———•———

Female, age 45.

First symptom: arthritis in hips and bone spurs. Made a truth at age seven when she felt unloved by her mother, who gave no support at home. She feared of getting recognition at school because mom would embarrass her. Mom talked about her in front of family members, humiliating her. Her truth: I am very angry from the lack of support or love from my mother and when I get attention from her it's negative.

Second symptom: stiff knees and fingers. Made a truth at age twelve when her mother wouldn't buy her any new clothes for school. Mom told her that clothes wouldn't cover up her face, saying, "No one will ever look at you the way your face looks (with acne). Clothes won't help you find a boyfriend." Her truth: Mom doesn't realize I have pride in my appearance and it's important to me. She doesn't care. How can she be so insensitive?

———•———•———

Female, age 27.

Symptom: keeps attracting scary relationships. At six, she was on a scary ride at the fair and cried out for it to stop. Her mom fussed at her for crying and being afraid. Her truth: whom do I trust? I can't trust my mom to help me when I am scared.

———•———•———

Female, age 37.

First symptom: feels like a second-class citizen with her boyfriend. Her mother seemed like Cruella de Vil when she was eight. She felt like she was getting unfair treatment for no reason. Her truth: Mom it makes me very angry to feel like an outsider, an intruder in my own home.

Second symptom: can't understand boyfriend's actions towards her. At age twelve, she told Mom that the gym teacher said she needed clothes that fit. Mom beat her. Her truth: You can't tell this woman the truth without getting whipped; dammed if I do, damned if I don't.

Third symptom: trouble with boyfriend's children. At age 13, her mom blamed her when her little brother was taken away because mom beat him. Her truth: I get blamed for doing the right thing: saving my little brother.

Fourth symptom: boyfriend nitpicking everything she does. At age 12, her mother berated her and complained about everything she did. Her truth: I get so angry with the way she treats me, no way on earth can I please this woman.

Fifth symptom: not getting recognition. When she was 12, her mom told her that her stepsister was pretty but she would never be anything but homely. Her truth: I never hear anything positive coming from Mom; I never get recognition and support from her.

———————

Male, age 45.

Symptoms: fear of loss, anger at God and Mom. When he was nine, his mother cut off all contact with paternal grandparents. It was a devastating loss. His truth: If you are real, God, you wouldn't have let Mom do this to me.

———————

Female, age 34.

Symptom: anger and rage with life and God. Made a truth at age thirteen when her mom wouldn't let her play drums in band; she had to play the saxophone because drums weren't ladylike. Her truth: It makes me mad Mom; you are always trying to control me. Where are you, God, when I need you?

Second symptom: life is not what I want it to be. At age 12, she was angry with her mom. Because of an appendix operation, she had to stay in bed and miss school activities. Her truth: my life is out of my control and nothing is going like I planned.

Third symptom: letting go of past relationships. At age 12, she realized her mother's traditional subservient lifestyle was nothing like she wanted. She had no interest in the kind of marriage like her mom. Her truth: You have to follow the rules set by society for being a woman or suffer the consequences.

———————

Female, 54.

First symptom: left hip pain. When she was seven, her mother had a nervous breakdown, staying in bed and crying all day long.

Her truth: I refuse to be weak like Mom; I can stand on my own if I have to.

Second symptom: low back trouble. Made a truth at age seven when her mother never came to church or school programs or gave any support to her. Her truth: Mom must not love me because of the way she treats me; actions speak louder than words.

Third symptom: hidden anger. When she was nine, her mother transferred her to another school so she could learn phonics. Her truth: It doesn't matter what I want; I never get to express anger at mom's actions.

------◄●——●►------

Summary:

Can you see the illusion in how they made their truths? It's not necessarily horrible things that cause us to make a truth; it's what we perceive as happening to us at the time. You as well as I have the same baggage of illusions stored as truths in our unconscious, waiting to rear its ugly head at lightening speed. I just want everyone to know that what we are reacting to in our daily life are emotions hiding behind the veil of the unconscious.

Ninety percent of the time when someone had angers at Mom, if you checked them for angers at God you would get a big "YES." That's a monumental reason to make peace with mom's presence or the memory of her presence. Being angry at God is counterproductive to a "Don't Worry! Be Happy!" existence.

This is just a smattering of the research I accumulated on attitudes toward mothers. There are many programs created by other people in our lives, but the record-holder is Mom. I only covered things before twenty years old, but trust me, we still make programs when we're fifty! I wanted you to have an idea of how programs from childhood, our "truth," still affect us daily. Our "truth" is only our "truth" just as our fingerprints are only our fingerprints. It's also why we need more than one session of letting go and forgiving to get to a place of peace within. Whew! It's a lot of emotional labor to forgive a circumstance that has become so personal to us. If you want to know more about the techniques of accessing the subconscious with Kinesiology, "muscle testing," visit <u>CoreHealth.us</u>.

9

Is Distance Healing A Pseudoscience?

YES AND NO

It is in some circles of belief, but not in mine. I have found that anything that can't be explained by modern science is much harder for the general public to accept. Being given the gift of sight, I can look in and see what is going on in the caller's field while talking to them on the phone when they need assistance in correcting their vibration. I get mixed views on my abilities. I've been told more than once that I may need to see a "special" doctor. Personally, I feel like you are not doing what you are supposed to do with your life unless you get a few eye-rolls, head shakes, and statements like: "You seem normal enough until you start to speak and we find out what you really do."

My job is to keep being real so I can assist other unusual people who have gifts that they don't know what to do with. It's like Christmas gifts we don't know what to do with; I have received a few of these and I would put them in the back of a cabinet because

I didn't want to offend anyone by giving them away. We treat our spiritual gifts the same way; we put them in the back of our minds and forget about them. You will find as you age that these gifts will call you and will want to be recognized. You will never feel complete until you set yourself free to be your authentic self.

It's hard on the psyche when we hide our spiritual abilities. We keep stumbling through the desert looking for an oasis, thinking that will be our savior; but that is only illusion. Our Soul will become a nuisance as it conjures up opportunities for us to experience our spiritual gifts. It's like trying to push a beach ball under water. It will pop to the surface at any second and will get your attention. You may as well give in and recognize what is coming to the surface; being in agreement with spiritual growth has fewer side effects. Until we embrace everything we are, we will never find true happiness and peace. Come out of the closet and set your gifts free and be your intuitive self!

A few years ago I was in Louisiana facilitating a workshop on "Meeting your Guides and Angels." After the first lecture on angels someone came to me with tears in her eyes, thanking me for letting her know that she wasn't crazy. Her family wouldn't allow her to talk about her ability to see things and she felt there was something wrong with her. This has happened over and over as damaged Souls find me for validation and healing. I have a close friend who suffered during her childhood because she could see through the dimensions of this world. They tried to have her institutionalized when she was a small child, because she was not normal. Thank God she lived through their ignorance and now she shares her gift by assisting others to bring forth their spiritual powers. I know one of these days you will get to see her on her own TV program. There is fame and recognition in her future.

Being my authentic self has helped many over the years as our spirits bumped into one another. Sometimes I am the seeker and these wonderful souls bring a message for me. I know I have been given the gift of communicating on many levels with wounded souls seeking direction. A large number of Indigo Children (children believed to possess supernatural abilities) were born between the years 1967-1984, and several began finding me when they reached their early twenties. These young adults came into the world with enhanced abilities and found that the third dimension wasn't the most favorable place to live. I worked with these lost souls that had turned to drugs and alcohol in order to cope with life. Most healers turned away from them, but something compelled me to give them love and support on their journey. In time they were able to accept who they were and now have normal Supernatural lives.

Question Number

10

Do I Need To Protect Myself While Sending Distance Healing?

CONSCIOUSNESS OF PROTECTION

I feel strongly that our protection comes from recognizing when we are unplugged from our source Light. I know in my heart that I am divinely protected from the malicious thoughts of others. I acknowledge that fear will be mine if I give it the power of belief. Knowing who I am and being my authentic self at all times is my best protection.

I know the world has anchored thought forms in the collective unconscious that are hard to overcome. They are made real by the fears of those not coming from a place of Oneness. Every time we feel powerless we give ourselves away to flawed thinking, to a thought form that is not necessarily true. Fear can hover in a place for centuries and every time we have the same frequency of fear we automatically plug into that vibe and we don't have to be in close proximity for it to happen. I am affected by watching the news. It will ruin my evening and screws with my consciousness. Some people love to watch TV programs about investigations of real people that were killed. I am the opposite! I like to watch programs like NCIS. I enjoy drama, but I don't want it about real people because I go there and get all tangled in their lives as the program unfolds. I start to feel what the people feel and it is quite uncomfortable for my psyche. Empathic people like myself need to realize that we have a different set of rules to live by.

If we are a low vibrational thinker we will plug into low vibrations. That's the main answer to the question, "How did I attract something like that into my life?" We are what we think! Whatever vibrates from our mind or our mouth connects to its twin frequency. Our vibration can never rise higher than our thoughts. No matter how much we wish for things to be different, they will never change until our consciousness changes. That's easy to accomplish if we are willing to go down a different path. It's like the old adage about the guy walking to work and falls down a hole in the road. He pulls himself out and goes on his way, thinking that tomorrow he will pay attention and not fall into the same pit. The next day he very carefully watches for the hole and steps around the edges. Day after day he vigilantly watches for the hole because he remembered how it hurt when he fell and what an effort it took to get out of the hole. Finally one day he becomes enlightened and decides to go a different route. We are like this man that does the same thing over and over being careful to always look for the pitfalls in life, thinking they will always be there waiting for us to make a mistake, until finally we realize we don't have to focus on what has happened. All we have to do is change directions and we are free of the burdens of believing life is one big hole waiting to swallow us up.

What I learned about protection the first years as a healer was to always be fearful of taking on someone else's pain or sickness. Yes, I took on others' pain and sickness at times because that was my belief. I definitely didn't have a true concept of Oneness. Belief is a powerful force when meshed with fear. I have found that like energies attract like energies; fear will align quickly with other fears until they don't. We stop the attraction of like frequencies by shifting our consciousness.

When we notice something different—a headache, a sudden uncomfortable feeling, pain, emotional sadness or anger—we have the opportunity to change the frequency. First we need to make sure we are grounded into the Universal Light as well as into Mother Earth ("As above, so below.") It brings balance back into our world when we connect to all fields of Light.

> *Use your body as a meter for registering a change in your field of Light.*

Recognizing that something is different is the first step in making a correction. You can initiate a beneficial program that alerts you when a lower frequency is about to invade your space. We have been creating programs ever since we were born and not all of them have been to our benefit, so why not install an intentional program that we can put to good use? Just take a conscious act and put it in motion and the subconscious will run with the new program. It has been installing programs for you that were not necessarily truth-oriented, but since they were your truth at the time, the subconscious obeyed your wishes. Why not work with the subconscious and install a more beneficial program that will assist you as you travel down your life's path? It will also assist in looking at programs that connect to a like frequency; the soul will see to that. While looking you can delete any program that is brought to your attention. It's the easy button!

DO I NEED A CRYSTAL OR AMULET TO PROTECT ME?

It is not necessarily true that you need a certain stone, crystal, amulet or incantation to be safe. I wear lots of stones and crystals and acknowledge that they contain a power within them. I love all my rocks, but I also know they are not necessary for my protection, if I believe in Oneness. What is true is the power of belief. "Belief in One Power." There is no separation from anything or anyone; we are divinely connected. Think about all the ways you have been taught to protect yourself. I have given many classes about protection using technique. We can feel a sense of powerlessness unless we adhere to the process we have chosen to protect us. Once we have become obligated to a particular formula we step out of our oneness and experience separation. If we believe just a little in the power of our "I AM" presence we are living our truth (your "I AM" presence is connecting and rising to the God in all of us). If God is Oneness and the only Power there is, then what have we to fear? Then the River of Truth flows through us and into the Universe as we take each breath.

Wear every stone and crystal that you have and place all the rocks you want around you, enjoying their frequency as it enhances yours. However, don't give power to your stone or crystal. If you believe that a stone can protect you, you believe in separation; separation from your true power of Oneness. What if you lost your protection or left it at home? What then? Are you at the mercy of the world because your crystal is not in your bra or pocket? These things alone are not necessary for your safety and protection. A connection to your Divine self is your protection. Everything else is the frequency of God being expressed through your belief.

IT'S THEIR JUNK!

We are the junk we emit into the Universe and it is mirrored back to us. Our junk seeks out and finds the same frequency of junk and blends the two frequencies, causing an amplification of the energies. "What do you mean, it's my junk?" You protest! "It's really not someone else's junk?" Well, no!

We like to think it's some evil presence, when we may be the perceived evil all along. We can establish coherence with convoluted Light just as easily as pure God Light. Self-righteous Light is tricky business and will shield you from the truth of your actions. We have to drop the pious attitude and start taking responsibility for our need to focus on the faults of others instead of addressing what is going on in our mind. I confess that I'm not perfect but I am trying to mend my wicked ways.

We are working from programs established in our Soul computers through our thoughts and the beliefs of others and the collective. Once these programs are activated, our Light plugs into frequencies we don't need to be plugged into at times. We are pure Light and the Light we emit attracts its twin. Sometimes the Light we emit has an embedded program that we are not aware of, acting like an arrow finding its target. Our main jobs are realizing it's just a running program, recognizing our part that is showing up in the program, and remembering we can change the program.

TAKING RESPONSIBILITY FOR OUR DR. FRANKENSTEIN CREATIONS

We are ruled by the subconscious. We like to think the conscious mind is in control, but it's not! We are ruled by that part of us that takes care of the unseen mechanics of our body. We never think about all the necessary things that our subconscious does for us. This same unconsciousness is in charge of all the programs we have installed in our Soul Computers and acts on its own volition without the conscious mind's approval. That's why we can deny that we had anything to do with what is going on right now. "I am as pure as the driven snow! No dirt here!"

Until we can see our part in what is happening in our life we will continue to have similar patterns appear causing even more dysfunction. We're usually not aware that it's our programs causing the dysfunction around us.

Your Soul is in charge of your dance card in life and wants you to experience whatever will assist with your evolution; the Soul works directly with the subconscious. If you haven't dealt with relationship issues your Soul will open your programs and keep bringing you the same frequencies with different names and faces until you acknowledge the part you are playing. If you have issues with money, or other people having money, you are operating from programs in your Soul computer and will keep having your lack of financial abundance validated over and over until you start to see a pattern. We will always be looking outside ourselves for Love/God -- someone or something to fill the empty hole in our heart/life. When we catch a glimpse of what is happening to our world and take responsibility for our creation, we allow change. That's when we take responsibility for all our Dr. Frankenstein creations, admitting we created the monsters that are anchored as truths in our subconscious.

WHAT IT ALL BOILS DOWN TO

The only protection we truly need is to believe there is no separation between us and God. When we can understand this statement nothing can touch us. What it means is that we have the truth of who we are carved into every cell in our body. When all the trillions of cells in our body function in Oneness we are there. Knowing who we are is essential to knowing our Oneness. Being whole and secure with how we look, how we love, with our job, with our dreams, fills in the chasm of separation.

I always expect to be protected, because it's my Divine Right. I give thanks for my protection and expect it to happen. When we understand that our thoughts produce an electromagnetic wave from the heart as they enter the electromagnetic field around us, which then connects us to everything in the Universe, we can understand the consequence of each thought. The Field reflects back to us whatever we send through our thoughts and spoken word. Caution here: spoken words travel at lightning speed in the Field and will manifest the outcome quickly. This is wonderful when everything that leaves our mind and mouth is positive, but scary, otherwise!

Smile more and have happier thoughts about your present state. Stop living in the past and stealing from the future, while expecting to produce a utopian state of living. Take responsibility for your happiness today, not after you get the new car or new front-loading washing machine and dryer.

Today is your gift, that's why it's called the present!

My Version Of How To Make The Magic Happen

SWEAT AND PAIN NOT REQUIRED FOR HAPPINESS

It's so simple to create happiness in our life that we find it hard to do! If I told you that your life could be magical and all your dreams come true if you would walk across a bed of hot coals while sticking needles in your fingers, you would probably do it. Why? We feel we don't deserve to be blessed if sweat and pain are not involved in the process. Growing up I remember hearing the quotes, "You gotta earn your salt!" Those beans just don't walk onto your dinner plate; hard work is part of the process. We hear things like this through our growing years from our parents, because that is what they heard. "Life is hard!"

It's time to break the process by changing those embedded beliefs; beliefs that are hardwired into our family line. I don't know about you, but I'm ready for the easy button. I'm not a big fan of suffering; in fact I don't like it and have decided not to experience it if at all possible. Let me tell you what I have learned as my "truth," and you are free to make it your "truth" if you want to jump on the same bandwagon.

ALEXANDRA'S TRUTH

You may think I have a head full of rocks, but I know better. I have proof it works! My life reflects my beliefs. You can take it with a grain of salt or swallow it whole; whatever makes you happy, because you get to choose.

Do you ever feel like there is a conspiracy going on and you are ruled from within by some shadow government? You say, "Surely I didn't create all the insanity that is going on in my world; it has to be the work of some malevolent influence." I really hate to burst your bubble, but look in the mirror and if there is any evil presence, it's the one staring back at you. We are the one who has plugged into some low vibrational energy that is affecting our world. We are the presence that plugs into all the insanity happening in our world and that same presence has the capabilities to create lots of wonderful experiences in our world by unplugging. Go back and read the section on cause and effect on page 56 if you need additional proof.

It all starts with the mind and what the mind is thinking. Whatever the mind is thinking, the heart is in agreement with, as each thought is processed through the heart. The heart opens programs according to the frequency of the thought. This may not seem important, but it is very important to have some understanding of the processes at work. During the process of mind/heart synchronization, the Soul comes on board because the Soul is sympathetic to the heart. The Soul carries the frequencies of our Sacred Contracts that we came into this lifetime to experience.

Here's more: each thought goes through the heart as well as the mind and when the activation takes place, it sends the message through the heart in an electromagnetic pulse and the heart sends the vibrational frequency into the electromagnetic field around us. Your thoughts will find their bull's eye impact point in the Field.

There is a sea of quantum fields that are connected to everything to which we are connected through infinity and beyond. We are connected to everyone on the planet through these fields and that's why distance healing is possible. That's also why it's easy to create a crappy life. Yes, we have all that fertilizer in the middle of our lives because of our thoughts plugging into their twin frequencies.

Our saintly affirmations can't change anything if our beliefs haven't changed. Remember, our subconscious is on board with every thought because of the heart connection and the heart works through the subconscious. It knows when we are telling the truth according to the programs we have installed. Now, the up side to that is that the subconscious will also believe us when we install a *new* truth. There is usually some forgiveness involved when dealing with past circumstances, when a new truth is created. I have found that if we address the past issue while in the quantum field, "Zero Point Energy," we have the ability to go beyond the past experience as we collapse the wave function that holds the construct. The wave function is the state of all possibilities, while the construct within the wave is the thought form of the observer. You can find lots of information about collapsing a construct by reading Richard Bartlett's book *The Physics of Miracles*. Dr. Bartlett created Matrix Energetics, a teachable way to access the Zero Point Field.

WHAT'S THE NEXT STEP?

Step into the arena of believing that we have some control over our little part of the universe. Know that whatever our mind can create has already happened and can be ours. When I sold Mary Kay Cosmetics almost 30 years ago, Mary Kay Ash told us, "If you believe it, you can achieve it!" She was right! Whatever goal I gave myself and believed it could be done, I did it. All you need is a belief the size of a grain of mustard seed, not a silo full of seeds. Matthew 17:20 says, "Verily I say unto you, if ye have faith of a grain of mustard seed, ye shall say unto this mountain, remove hence to yonder place; and it shall remove; and nothing shall be impossible unto you" (The Bible, KJV). If we believe, we can move mountains; think about those possibilities as the wave is collapsing into particles.

Creation has begun once your belief leaves your mind; simultaneously, an electromagnetic pulse leaves your heart, entering the electromagnetic field around you carrying the code. When the code enters the field, it finds its mate and will connect just like the halo connections in the movie *Avatar*. It works like magic every time—I'm not talking David Copperfield magic; I'm talking Merlin kind of magic. You will find yourself standing with the wand in your hand as your dream materializes before you.

It's really science at work or you could call it the magic of science. The side effects of Spiritual Technology are all about belief and where we park our mind. When we gaze at the wave function we engage with the particles within the wave and when the wave collapses we have the opportunity to create. Know that the construct present within the wave is our creation, we made it! The truth is you can choose the red pill or the blue pill; it's totally up to you, Alice. Our choices determine our experiences. Now this is something we should try to understand just a little: we made the construct. If we have the ability to construct, we also have the ability to *re-construct*. When we look at any situation, we are constructing according to our belief in what we observe. Whatever we think, good or bad, happy or sad, we are creating.

Think back to your last judgmental appraisal of a situation, when you knew you were right and others were wrong. How much effect did your judgment have? Did they change because you judged them? Did they come and thank you for your self-righteous beliefs? Probably not! Before you judge, step into the moccasins of the one being judged and observe it from their point of view.

LET'S SUMMARIZE

We create through the choices we make and the consequences of those choices will broadcast in our world. Whatever we believe, we can achieve. All we have to do is believe that anything is possible, while staying out of the business of someone else's life, especially those who live in the same house with us.

It's hard to accomplish only because we tend to point an unruly finger at others. This delinquent appendage assists the subconscious in bringing hidden beliefs to the surface. Stop blaming others by pointing a finger in their direction for whatever has gone wrong in your world. Take responsibility for the calamities showing up and know that it's just programs running. When you recognize it's a program running you can delete the program and create another more beneficial program. FYI: consequences might stop being our constant companion if we kept our hands in our pockets.

I have found that loving someone without wanting to change them is the most powerful element for change that you can muster on this planet. If we love others just for the joy of loving, walls crumble and storms subside. If we see them as lovable they can see themselves as lovable. What a marvelous gift to give and receive!

Put out your hand and plug into the matrix around you; become a part of a living, breathing system of unlimited potential. Being consciously aware that you have plugged into a system of Divine Intelligence will allow you to be the creator of your dreams. When we let go of our beliefs and subscribe only to the journal of love, we can create Shangri-La.

Mind your own business. Learn to recognize the difference between a program running and a nuclear attack. Own the fact that you are the malicious energy at play in your life and not some outside force causing the chaos. Be willing to forgive your shortcomings as you forgive the shortcomings of others. Be your authentic self every day on planet earth and happiness will be yours.

Last but not least: turn to love as your first resort.

How to Pray

Before you get a bag of rocks to throw, hear me out. We have the mistaken belief that we must beg and plead for God to hear and assist us when there is a need. This is programmed into our psyche by the well-meaning teachings of our family and spiritual leaders. You may want to call me a heretic when you read how I feel and that's OK, because I would have felt the same way years ago. I prayed for God's help and assistance every day. When my prayers weren't answered I prayed harder for more assistance.

When we pray asking God for things we are initiating cause and effect. Asking means we believe in separation, whether we know it or not. If we believe there is a need to request favors from God, we believe that God is not a real part of our lives. God is outside of our life and we keep looking for the doorbell to ring. As Joel Goldsmith reveals, pray for the sake of praying, realizing God and nothing more. When we realize God we are bringing God into every molecule of our existence. We already have everything that we could possible imagine, it's already ours even before we ask. All we have to do is align and say, "Thank you, God, that I am so blessed to be the owner of so much Love." Instead we pray, "God, will you please pay my phone bill? God, will you smite that person at work who is giving me grief? God, will you ever give me enough money for a new car? I keep praying while driving my old rattletrap. God, I really like Joey; can you make him like me?" If this kind of prayer is not working for you and your life is still a jumble of one erratic moment after another, maybe you should try something different.

THE PROCESS

Sit quietly, breathe easily, smile and see God sitting beside you or better still, see yourself meshed inside of God. That is the true image that says there is no separation. Think about it: God knows your every thought, your every wish, and your every concern. Why do you presume you need to inform God of something that is already known? Isn't that like being the nagging child? When you go to your refrigerator to get something to eat do you ask permission to eat the food? No, because you went to the store and paid for the groceries and they are yours. Isn't it silly to ask yourself if you can eat your food? Isn't it just as silly to ask God for things that have already been given to you? It's your responsibility to believe in the omnipotent awesomeness of God. You have already been blessed with everything you could possibly need and now it's time to align.

ALIGNING

Being in agreement with everything that is in motion around you at all times teaches you about aligning to God. If we realize that everything, even the not-so-perfect moments, is God-infused, we can see the real picture being painted in the moment. Then take a breath and allow the Spirit of God to finish the masterpiece.

Do you really, honest-to-God know what you want in this life? Do you have a visual in your mind that you can conjure up at any time about how you want your life to be? We need to have the architect's drawing of our wishes and dreams, not the completed house. Just a snippet will do. Then we turn the plans over to God and *sit*, realizing God knows all things that we need. Now let it go and stop nagging God. The Spirit of God takes care of the business of aligning your Light to the appropriate Light to bring forth every wish you have.

This works! I have proof that it works! You can make it work in your world also, if you give the power of creation back to God.

Glossary of Terms

Family Entity: The Family Entity is built by the beliefs threaded through our family line. It gains substance from years of dogmatic beliefs held in place by the power of myth. "This is how our family has always done it and how we have survived all these years." The purpose of the ancestral line is to guard its pure heritage. The Family Entity takes on a life of its own and will be present during any occurrence that is energetically threaded through the Family Line. Anything that has a contrary frequency concerning the Family Line will be dealt with by the Family Entity. To be in harmony with the Family Entity you must obey the mindset of the family and not become an individual mind. When we express our individuality we are met with resistance.

However, once we become our authentic self and truly know who we are, we can make peace with the Family Entity and be allowed to have our own beliefs as truths.

Higher Consciousness/ Superconscious Mind: Is the truly enlightened part of us that has all the answers, to every question you can imagine. It has infinite intelligence since it is the mind of God (the Universal Mind), that is connected to everything. The part of us that makes good decisions and connects us to every opportunity our mind can devise. It sets things in motion for our alignment with the right people to appear in our life, at the right time, making room for opportunities to manifest. This highest aspect will assist as lessons unfold when necessary for our spiritual growth. When we give our goals to this highest aspect it will respond quickly. Everything will unfold according to our belief in the dream. Once we truly understand the superconscious mind power of the Higher Self, we will realize that being successful has nothing to do with being lucky in life.

Inner Planes: A place where time is nonexistent; a place where the Divine Principles of God reside. Gregg Braden would call it the Divine Matrix. Everything is fluid on the Inner Planes. You can go to the past as easily as going to the future and look at any circumstance in your life or the lives of others. The avenue to anything you wish to see is located on the Inner Planes. It is accessed during the Alpha state, a self-hypnotic state, similar to driving home and not remembering the complete journey.

You can connect easily to the Soul Light of others on the Inner Planes, communicating on a Soul's level to send healing energies or messages of forgiveness. The Spiritual Technology of distance healing works through the Inner Planes.

Out-picturing: This is the evidence of our thinking manifested before us in real time. Whatever is showing up in our world today is whatever we put in motion yesterday. It's something that can't be hidden from us; it will be out in the open and in our face to see. If we think that having enough money to pay our bills requires hard work, we will see it out-picture in our lives as having two jobs and stacks of unpaid bills on the table.

Our hostility to friends and family will outpicture as separation in our world. The actions we take towards others will always be reflected back to us with the same vibrational frequency code being sent. If we are sending unconditional love we receive unconditional love from others.

Supernatural Power: The ability to use the gifts of psychic powers by accessing other realms of energies that do not exist in the consciousness of the ordinary individual. Anything that is not explained by the laws of physics can be labeled Supernatural. Above and beyond what is natural.

Remote viewing, medium ship, psychic healing, clairvoyance are a few examples of Supernatural Powers.

Universal Light: the Great Sea of Universal Light, Life, and Love. *Unveiled Mysteries* **states:**

"Try to think upon this Power, which is within you. Call into use the Great Sea of Universal Substance from which you may draw without limit. It obeys, without exception, the direction of thought, and records any quality imposed upon it, through the activity of the feeling nature in mankind. Universal Substance is obedient to your conscious will at all times. It is constantly responding to humanity's thought and feeling whether they realize it or not. There is no instant at which human beings are not giving this Substance one quality or another, and it is only through the knowledge that the individual has conscious control and manipulation of a Limitless Sea of It that he begins to understand the possibilities of his own Creative Powers, and the responsibilities resting upon him in the use of his thought and feeling."

Wikipedia: *en.wikipedia.org/wiki/Ascended_Master_Teachings*

Zero Point Energy/Divine Matrix/Zone: Vacuum energy is the zero-point energy of all the fields in space, which in the Standard Model includes the electromagnetic field, other gauge fields, fermionic fields, and the Higgs field. It is the energy of the vacuum, which in quantum field theory is defined not as empty space but as the ground state of the fields.

Zero-point energy - Wikipedia, the free encyclopedia

Wikipedia:en.wikipedia.org/wiki/Zero-point_energy

Copyrights

Excerpts from *The Thunder of Silence, "Cause and Effect" by* Joel S. Goldsmith, Copyright ©1961 Harper and Row

Invisible Gorilla test, test, conducted by Daniel Simons of the University of Illinois at Urbana-Champaign and Christopher Chabris of Harvard University. This study, a revised version of earlier studies conducted by Ulric Neisser, Neisser and Becklen, 1975 http://*en.wikipedia.org/ wiki/Inattentional_blindness August, 2011 July 2012*

Excerpts of article from the book "Zero Limits" by Dr. Joe Vitale and Dr. Len on Joe Vitale website *www.mrfire.com/article.../**new**-articles/ worlds-most-unusual-therapist.html* copyright 2005

Excerpt from Dr. Joe Vitale's website on Dr. Ihaleakala Hew Len, The World's Most Unusual Therapist. From "Zero Limits" by Joe Vitale and Dr. Hew Len, Balboapress

CPSIA information can be obtained at www.ICGtesting.com
Printed in the USA
LVOW10s0158021014

406803LV00005B/12/P